LON

London's Gone

J. M. Evans

DERNIER PUBLISHING
Tonbridge

Copyright © J. M. Evans 2006

First published 2006

Published by Dernier Publishing
P.O. Box 403, Tonbridge, TN9 9BJ, England
www.dernierpublishing.com

ISBN (13-digit)   978 0 9536963 2 1
ISBN (10-digit)   0 9536963 2 4

All rights reserved.
No part of this publication may be reproduced or
transmitted in any form or by any means, electronic
or mechanical, including photocopy, recording or any
information storage and retrieval system, without
permission in writing from the publisher.

Cover illustration by Maureen Carter

Book design and production for the publisher by
Bookprint Creative Services, P.O. Box 827, BN21 3YJ, England.
Printed in Great Britain.

London's Gone

one

Mum and Dad should have been back hours ago. Their beautifully restored country home now lay dark and cold; the only light came from the thin, blue beam of Maria's torch. Maria and Emily were alone. Maria was tired, angry and tense with the fear that had started living in her stomach. She stood in the doorway of Emily's bedroom, glaring fiercely at her younger sister through the shadows. "I'm not asking you, Emily, I'm telling you – if Mum and Dad aren't back by morning, we're going to Granny and Grandpa's." At 16 years old Maria was strikingly attractive, with short, dark hair and a pretty face. She also had a determined air, which Emily, the younger by two years, could not match.

There was a tense pause. Emily looked up at her sister from her fluffy pink beanbag seat, her pale face reflecting the dread that Maria felt but refused to show. "But we can't go," she objected. "Mum said we had to stay here till they got back from fetching Granny and Grandpa." Her voice wavered and she quickly wiped away a tear before it fell. Her long, fair hair hung loose, unkempt.

Maria stood there fuming, her dark eyes blazing with anger and hidden fear. Why did little sisters have to be so infuriating? As if there weren't enough problems! "I know they told us to wait here, Stupid, but they said they'd be back in a couple of hours – that was at breakfast! Something's gone wrong – maybe one of them is ill or something. We can't just wait here for ever!"

"But it could be dangerous!"

"Dangerous or not, we're going." There was a pause, heavy in the suffocating, silent darkness.

"How are we going to get there?" Maria relaxed a little. Emily was giving in.

"We'll cycle. I've checked the bikes. They're OK."

"But that will take ages!" lisped Emily through her brace. "What if . . ." Her lower lip trembled, and new tears started to trickle down her cheeks. "What if we get there . . . and they're not there?" Maria closed her eyes in exasperation.

"Then we come back of course!"

"If they come back tonight, we won't have to go?"

"You're very quick."

"But . . . suppose we miss them?"

"We leave a note, so they know where we are."

"But what if . . ."

"Oh shut up with your 'what ifs', Em," snapped Maria.

"But what if Mum and Dad go to the cottage without us?" continued Emily, wiping away the tears that carried on dripping down her pale face.

"Oh for goodness sake stop blubbing, you know they wouldn't leave their precious little Emily! Of course they wouldn't go without us – without you, anyway." Maria could feel the irrational anger rising to hide her own fears.

"We've got to go and see what's happened to them. It'll only take a couple of hours, max."

"I don't want to go," said Emily stubbornly, through her tears. "I know Mum and Dad will be back."

"You don't know, you hope!" retorted Maria, losing her grip on the rising tide of her emotions. "They might even be dead for all you know!" That finished Emily off. She ran out of the room past Maria, sobbing and slammed the bathroom door behind her.

Maria was shocked at her own words. Maybe their parents really were dead. That thought had been hovering at the back of her mind, but saying it seemed to make it more possible somehow . . . Yesterday, she didn't even like them. That was yesterday. She walked slowly to her own bedroom, sank down on to her bed and looked round in the darkness, her emotions reeling. Here was everything she had wanted; widescreen telly with DVD, CD player, the best speakers . . . but it didn't mean anything now. None of it worked, anyway, without electricity. Maria shivered. Fear, anguish, misery and a feeling of being utterly alone swept over her and as there was nobody to see, she allowed her own silent tears to fall.

* * *

Just one day since the bombing. One long, long day.

Maria had watched those awful planes slice up the gentle March day, with her family. They were at their home, just a few miles from Sonbridge in the picturesque Kent countryside. The girls had not long returned from school. Dad, who despite having a leg in plaster was trying to do some gardening on his day off, had excitedly shouted to everyone to run out and look at the planes. He thought they were practising for an air display. How stupid! At six o'clock on a Tuesday evening! To assert her independence, Maria hadn't gone out, but she had watched from her bedroom window.

The sinister cloud of black war planes had swept low over the North Downs like an angry swarm of demons. They had seemed to rip the sun and sky to shreds as they tore overhead. The deafening scream of the engines was terrifyingly exhilarating – Maria had had to put her hands over her ears; even the house had shuddered in protest. She saw her family laughing in the garden below, with their hands over their ears too. And, in just a few seconds, the planes had gone.

Then they had dropped their deadly cargo on London. On London! It was so unfair! Everyone knew about terrorists, but nobody had said that this could happen. There had been no warning, nothing. Nothing but the planes. Maria shivered as she remembered the distant explosions echoing over the valley. The very hills shook, as if recoiling in terror at what was being done to them. Maria's family had all watched the mushroom of smoke rising from the direction of London in silent horror. The grey cloud had ascended like an evil genie, powerful and triumphant. Then the demon planes had returned; empty, black and evil, screaming victory. It had felt like a dream, a nightmare.

Maria had joined the others in the orange-and-white

kitchen. She hated the colour scheme and didn't like her family much, but for once she didn't want to be alone. Mum tried to make a cup of tea, but there was a power cut, so she poured glasses of apple juice instead. In the far distance they could hear the sirens of emergency vehicles and the whirr of helicopters. "God knows what they'll find," muttered Dad, shaking his head in disbelief. Mum raised her eyebrows. That meant, "Not in front of the girls." But they had both heard him, anyway.

The phones and the TV were dead. Mum searched for and found an old radio in the cupboard under the stairs, to try to get some news. The batteries were weak – amazing that they worked at all – but there was just an awful crackling noise where most of the channels should have been. Mum persevered. Everyone tried their mobile phones, but there was no signal. Mr Kingsley-Brown, the family's only neighbour, came round and talked quietly in a corner with Dad for a few minutes, then after shaking hands with Dad as if he might never see him again, he zoomed off in his shiny red Porsche.

Maria sat in shocked silence with Emily at the breakfast bar, wishing she hadn't lent her iPod to Michelle, listening to the ghastly rising and fading of the crackling on the radio as Mum tried to find a clear signal. A thousand thoughts jumbled through her mind. Was this the beginning of a real war? What was going to happen now? A couple of hours ago she had been on the bus with her friends! Could life really change this much in such a short time? Lots of people must have died . . . She was waiting for it all to end, or to wake up, or for Dad to laugh and tell them that it was all just a joke, that it wasn't real.

But suddenly a voice on the radio was real, and out of the confusion came reports of central London being razed to the ground. London – nothing but a pile of bricks.

two

Mum and Emily had cried and Dad's face was grim as they listened to what news there was over the next hour. "Thousands of people are thought to have lost their lives in the London bombing," announced the solemn voice over the radio. "Emergency services and hospitals on the outskirts of London are preparing themselves to receive casualties, although widespread power failure is causing severe disruption . . ." Maria felt blank, empty, apart from a knot of fear inside. She fiddled with a magazine, pretending not to listen, but hearing every word.

There was no music, just report after report, like a radio play that wouldn't end. "The Queen is understood to be safe at Sandringham. What we can confirm is that the Prime Minister, along with many leading government figures, was in Westminster at the time of the bombing and is unlikely to have survived the attack. Middle East Peace Talks may have been the target . . ." From time to time the reports were interspersed with angry denunciations by various world leaders. "We condemn in the strongest way violence of this appalling nature . . .", "We will spare no effort in seeking out and apprehending the murderers who carried out this atrocity . . ." Then there was news from a helicopter, circling the ruins of central London. The reporter's voice seemed far away, unreal above the whirring of the helicopter blades. "London's gone!" exclaimed the man. "It is an unbelievable picture from up here . . . all one can see for mile after mile is dust, smoke, fire, buildings burning and rubble . . . little is recognisable . . . the Houses of Parliament and Buckingham Palace, appear to have received direct hits . . . we can just make out the twisted remains of the London Eye, choking the Thames . . ."

The reports were relentless. Violence began to break out in some of the larger cities as people took to the streets in panic. Shops were being smashed, looted and set on fire by gangs of youths and thousands of people were beginning to flee the country, jamming the roads to the coast as airports closed. Then there were awful rumours of the planes returning to other cities with chemical weapons; deadly gases that could devastate a whole nation within a week.

Dad shook his head. "I'm sure they won't do that, it's against the Geneva Convention," he muttered. All the same, he got up a little while later and went round the house, stopping up cracks in the doors and windows. The rest of them just sat there, listening, waiting.

Nobody seemed to know where the planes had come from, but an extreme Middle Eastern terrorist group was suspected. What better way to get rid of all their enemies' leaders in one go?

Dad got up, went over to the window and muttered something about "terrorist cowards". Mum went over to him and they hugged. Maria pretended to study her magazine. They never did that, not in front of them, anyway. It was Emily who voiced her fears.

"Is this a war? Are we going to die?" she asked in a small, scared voice, lisping through her brace.

"No, of course not," said Dad, far too loudly. "I don't know what's going on, but we've got America and the rest of Europe to rely on, so don't worry, we'll just have to sit tight and wait for help. Now it's all over we'll be safe here." He smiled with his mouth, but not with his eyes, and Maria looked away. Nobody else bothered to talk after that.

It was about an hour later that the batteries in the radio faded away. Mum found some more in the electronic battleships game, but they only lasted a few minutes before the woman's voice disappeared into nothing. In a way it was a relief.

Then there was just silence and the growing darkness. Dad fetched some candles from the lounge and lit them. At Christmas they had seemed to give a cosy glow, but now their light seemed cold and cheerless. The house was cold too, but the heating didn't work. Emily helped Mum to make some sandwiches, but nobody was hungry. Dad searched in the garage for the camping stove so they could at least have a hot drink, then, as there was nothing else to do, they went to bed.

"We'll all feel better in the morning," said Mum, trying to smile, as she handed out extra blankets by candlelight. Nobody said anything, but they knew she was lying. They might even be dead. Emily gave her a hug. Maria went to her room.

She stood in the doorway, shivering a little in the cold. It hardly seemed like her room; the candle she was carrying gave an eerie light, which made the green walls ghostly and the shadowy corners look as if they held dark secrets. Even the celebrities on the posters seemed to leer at her rather than smile and they jumped about in the flickering light as if possessed by demons. "Adam, save me," she begged her idol, the adorable Adam Johanssen from the hit group "Slash", but he ignored her. His blue eyes just kept staring down at her in the half-light as if nothing had happened. "Don't you know we're in trouble?" implored Maria. Then she remembered that he was on tour in the USA. At least he was alive; that was a comforting thought. Maria took a grip on herself. If Adam had survived, she had to survive too.

She started to undress for bed, then changed her mind. Suppose something happened in the night? She would sleep in her clothes. To start with it would be warmer, but also, if they had to leave in a hurry for any reason, she wouldn't have to rush out in her pyjamas. How embarrassing would that be? She chose a pair of black trousers and a soft jumper from her wardrobe and pulled on a pair of socks. Maybe, if they did have to leave, they would go to their summer cottage on the coast. And even if they stayed at home, they might get a few days off school . . . Despite everything, Maria grinned to herself. Boy, would her teachers be glad to have time off without her! She would miss her friends though, Mad Michelle and Trusty Trudi – what a team they made! The tricks they played on Miss Gunn, their gullible form tutor! What a gang! Maybe she would never see them again. That was an awful thought, but she brushed it away quickly . . . unlikely! Imagine anyone letting you off school for more than a few days, especially with exams looming up. And if she was alive, her friends were sure to still be around.

Maria started to pack a few things. If they did have to leave in a hurry, she wasn't going to be unprepared — she'd show everyone how organised she was. And anyway, there was no way she was going to go anywhere without make-up and a hairbrush at the very least — you never knew when you might meet the man of your dreams . . .

It was good to be doing something. Maria caught herself humming as she dumped the school books out of her backpack and replaced them with a change of clothes, a pair of trainers, her make-up bag and hairbrush, then went to the bathroom to collect some essential toiletries. She took her candle with her, laughing at herself for thinking that the room had looked spooky. Now that she was doing something with a purpose, Maria felt quite cheerful. She went downstairs to fetch her jacket from the hall cupboard. It was quite an adventure really, this plane business! If everything worked out well, they would get an extended holiday — plus they would be sure to take Granny and Grandpa with them, which would be cool. They were so much more fun than boring interior decorator Mum and nothing-matters-but-work doctor GP Dad! Her parents didn't seem to like her much, but her grandparents did. Somehow, they understood things. Granny had been a rebel in her school days and had once even set her teacher's desk on fire; Maria admired her for that! And Grandpa was always so cheerful. His jokes were awful, but he had one of those infectious laughs; nobody could help but laugh when he laughed. Maria half-wondered how they were, but she knew that they would be fine; they would pray and their prayers always worked. Anyway, they were further away from London than they were, near Dad's surgery in the centre of town.

On the way back to her room with her jacket, Maria heard Mum and Dad talking in the lounge, at first in hushed whispers, then sounding more desperate. They were supposed to have gone to bed! She crept up to the crack in the door to listen. It sounded as if they were having an argument. "Ursula, I know I don't work at the hospital," she heard her father say fiercely, "but they'll need all the help they can get! It's my duty to do what I can, don't you see?"

"No, no, please, Brian, you must stay with us," she heard her mother beg. Then there was silence. Mum was crying. Maria crept back to her room. Dad wanted to leave them. His stupid patients were more important than them, as usual, thought Maria bitterly. Her cheerful mood crumbled. She finished packing her bag in a more sombre mood, then looked out of the bedroom window, for the first time since the afternoon – since the planes. There were no stars, just cloud. Or dust. The thought of it containing the ashes of thousands of people was almost too much to bear. Maria felt sick and she shivered, not just with the cold. The knot of fear in her belly returned.

three

Maria had intended to keep the candle alight on her bedside cupboard for a while, just for the fun of it, but its flickering got on her nerves, so she blew it out. Not that the darkness brought any comfort. At any time she expected something to happen, although she didn't know what. She tossed and turned, jumping at the slightest noise, desperate to escape the haunting visions of the planes and the smoke rising from London, but sleep laughed in her face. It mocked her thoughts and jumbled up all her unanswerable questions. Why hadn't the planes been stopped? Would they come back? What was going to happen now? Would Dad leave them? What do chemical weapons do to you?

At last, in the early hours of the morning, Maria drifted off into an exhausted sleep. But even then it didn't bring the relief of oblivion, it brought with it a confusion of dark thoughts: gangs of menacing youths, shops on fire, people crying out in pain and a pall of smoke which sounded like war planes and seemed to get bigger and bigger until it reached her and swallowed her up. She tried to cry out and escape from its unyielding grip – but it was Mum shaking her.

"Get up, Maria, we need to talk," she urged her. Maria groaned. Relief at ending the nightmare was mixed with a deep weariness.

"What's happened? What time is it? It's still dark," she grumbled, pulling the duvet closer round her ears to blot out the fear from the nightmare, which didn't want to let her go.

"It's only six o'clock, darling, but there are things we need to discuss. Come down to the kitchen as quick as you can." Mum sounded determined, which was unusual. Maria groaned and rolled out of bed. She knew what would happen. There wouldn't be a discussion; Dad would tell her what to do, she wouldn't want to do it, they would have an argument, she would get a punishment and everyone would be in a bad mood. But at least she was alive and the planes hadn't come back – not yet, anyway.

Dad looked solemn when Maria made it to the breakfast table. There were bags under his eyes, Maria noticed, which matched the colour of the stubble on his chin. He obviously hadn't slept much. Emily's peaky face and large eyes were staring into space. There was a welcome smell of coffee, thanks to the camping stove, but just a plate of marmalade sandwiches and cereal with lukewarm milk for breakfast. Maria took a mouthful of cornflakes, then pushed the bowl away in disgust. "Gross, warm milk, you can forget that," she sniffed. "I'll just have coffee."

Dad ignored her and poured her some coffee. He and Mum exchanged a look, which Maria translated as, "Just ignore her." That was worrying. She had expected a shouting match. She tried again. "I hope you've got a good reason for dragging me out of bed at this hour of the morning," she said loudly, heaping sugar into her coffee for extra effect. "I never get up at six o'clock. It doesn't suit me."

"Sorry, love," said Mum, avoiding her eyes. "Only we've had to make some very important decisions, and we need to let you girls know what's going on." She looked up and smiled – the sort of smile she used for her clients, minus the pink lipstick. Maria didn't smile. It really is bad, she thought to herself. The niggling fear inside grew a little larger and she shut up.

"I went out to the car in the night," Dad began to explain, "to listen to the radio." He paused. "The news isn't good. There could be a war. News is sparse, but people are being warned to get away from the big cities. Manchester may be next, Birmingham, who knows?" Dad put his head in his hands. "Our own military are apparently on red alert, but with the government gone, there's confusion. Also," he continued tiredly, wiping his forehead with a handkerchief, "there are reports of gangs, who went out last night in the suburbs of London, burning, looting and . . . well, just doing what they wanted. They're angry, of course. Lots of them have lost family, homes . . . But we need to get away, we're too close to London. Nobody's saying they will come here," he added quickly, hearing Emily's gasp of fear, "but it's better to be safe than sorry. We'll go to the cottage until it's safe to come back." He looked at the two girls, Emily white-faced and shaken, Maria pretending not to care.

"Won't you volunteer your services at the hospital?" she asked her father, trying to sound nonchalant, although her heart was thumping. "Think of all those poor, injured people!" Her sarcasm was either lost or ignored.

"My first duty is towards my family," he replied briskly.

"Well, I thought we'd go to the cottage," said Maria airily, trying not to show how relieved she was that he wasn't deserting them. She might not like him much, but he was her dad. "I've already packed a few things. When do we leave?" She turned and smiled mockingly at Emily. "An extra holiday!"

"It's not as easy as that, love," said Dad. "We're going to take your grandparents with us, so the first thing is to go and fetch them."

Maria and Emily nodded. Cool, thought Maria. Just as she'd thought. This could turn out to be fun! It would be safe at the cottage and they could forget about the troubles. There would be no school, Dad was never as mean when Granny and Grandpa were around . . . Maria smiled to herself as she stirred her coffee. She could look forward to some excellent clubbing at Callum and there probably wouldn't be a war. Things like that only happen to other people. She made a mental note to pack her favourite strappy top.

"As you know, I can't drive with my leg in plaster," continued Dad, "so Mum needs to drive. But as we're passing near my surgery, I'm going to stop off and pick up some medical supplies. They may well come in useful.

The only thing is, we can't all go, there isn't room in the car. We're going to have to leave you girls on your own for a couple of hours."

Emily gasped. "Can't we come too?"

"We won't all fit in one car," Mum repeated quietly. "We'll bring Granny and Grandpa back in my Peugeot, then we'll take both cars to the cottage. Grandpa can drive Dad's Mercedes. You girls can go with him if you like!"

"OK," said Maria, sipping her coffee. Mum smiled encouragingly, but Emily didn't smile back.

"Dad could stay and you could get his stuff," persisted Emily, "or Dad could go later with Grandpa, couldn't he?"

"Emily, we've thought it all through carefully," said Mum gently. "Dad needs to get his medical things himself – I wouldn't have a clue – and we must fetch Granny and Grandpa at the same time. We have to be careful with petrol, it might not be easy to get any more for a while." Mum went over to Emily's chair and put an arm round her shoulders. "It'll be OK, darling, we won't be long." She stroked Emily's hair and kissed her forehead.

Yuck, thought Maria. Mummy's little baby. She made a disgusted face in their direction. It wasn't fair, she thought. Why doesn't Mum say nice things to me? She'd show them she didn't care.

"Why don't you take Emily with you?" she suggested loftily, putting on an affected smile and starting a sandwich. "You've got room for her. She's only little. You can leave me, I don't mind." She forced the thought of chemical weapons and the gangs of angry people deep down until she couldn't feel it. There was a moment's silence. Maria noticed how tired both her parents looked. They weren't really that old, but both of them looked wrinkled and grey and Dad's shoulders stooped as he sat at the table. Mum and Dad exchanged a glance. Emily looked unsure. She obviously wanted to go.

"Look, Maria love," said Dad. "Honestly, we've thought it through. It's very brave of you, but we don't want to leave you alone."

Maria shrugged her shoulders. "Suit yourselves. It's all the same to me." She tried to look normal, but inside she felt sick. She realised with disgust that she was glad that Emily was staying – despite the bravado, she didn't want to be alone.

"Anyway," said Mum, breezily getting up and clearing the breakfast things away, "don't worry, everything will be fine. It's just five miles there and five miles back. We'll stop long enough to help Granny and Grandpa pack a few things, but even so we should only be an hour or two. While you're waiting for us, pack your own bags. One suitcase each, OK? Don't answer the door to anybody and don't use the stove, we don't want any fires." Mum noticed Emily's worried face and gave her a hug. "Don't worry, love, everything will be fine. Just wait here till we get back."

The scrunch of tyres on the pebbled drive seemed to hang in the cold, misty morning air for a moment, while the roar of the engine faded in the distance. Then both were extinguished. Silence fell on the house like a thick, grey blanket. Maria felt like she was being abandoned – dumped and left. Her stomach churned. This is what it's like when something awful happens, thought Maria. It wasn't nice. She went and made herself another coffee, on the stove.

four

That day seemed as if it would never end. Maria usually drowned out silence, anger and boredom with music – without electricity or her iPod she couldn't do that. Outside, the sun was breaking through the clouds and a warm sunny breeze teased the golden daffodils, but Maria was in no mood to enjoy the wonders of creation. All morning she packed, unpacked and re-packed the biggest suitcase she could find, which helped the time to pass, but the "hour or two" Mum had mentioned came and went with no sign of her parents' return. Maria could hear Emily moving about the house, but she left her to her own devices. So what if she was worried. Silly Mummy's baby! But as the hours went by – three, four, then five – Maria became increasingly worried and angry herself. How dare their parents leave them like this? Emily at least had a right to be looked after!

Eventually Maria left her room on the pretext of getting some lunch, although really she wanted some company. Her sister was hardly her ideal choice of person, but Maria had to grudgingly admit that even she was better than nobody. Emily came out of the sun lounge on hearing Maria go downstairs. "Why do you think Mum and Dad are being so long?" she asked. Maria played it cool. She shrugged nonchalantly.

"How should I know?"

"Do you think they'll be long?"

"Haven't a clue."

"What are we going to do?"

"Wait. What else?" Emily's questions were making Maria uncomfortable, although she was reluctant to lose her company. "Want some lunch?" she asked.

"OK." Emily followed Maria into the kitchen. Maria hummed as she cut thick slices from a loaf of bread, as if everything was normal.

"The butter's soft!" she said. "The fridge is off." She made a face as she sniffed the ham. "Oh gross, the ham's gone off."

"Why is the fridge off – does it run on electricity?" asked Emily.

"Of course it does, are you stupid or what? What do you want in your sandwich?"

"Ham and tomato."

"I said, Stupid, the ham's off."

"How do you know? It might not be."

In exasperation, Maria couldn't help herself. She peeled off the top layer of ham and threw it at Emily. "Here, try it and see!" The pink slice landed neatly on Emily's face and stuck there for a second, like an extra skin. Maria burst into peals of laughter. Emily was furious.

"Don't throw that at me, it stinks!" she yelled.

"Told you it was off!"

Emily snatched the ham off her face and hurled it

furiously back in Maria's direction. Maria dodged, but the fragile slice broke into several pieces, one of which landed on her trousers, making a greasy mark. "Look what you've done!" she gasped, picking off the offending piece of meat. "You've asked for it now!" Maria began to throw the remaining ham at Emily, slice by slice, grinning wickedly. A ham fight – now that was a first! Emily screamed, dodged and tried to dart out of the door, but Maria cut her off, so she started to chuck the meat back. Even Emily started to laugh, getting into the swing of it. It was hilarious to watch the ham fly through the air – it wobbled and landed just where it was least expected! One particularly good aim of Emily's landed on Maria's head. Emily creased up, pointing at her triumph. Maria found she had run out of ammunition, so she grabbed a tub of cottage cheese, stuck her fingers in and pulled out a handful. "You've asked for this!"

"No!" shrieked Emily, backing up against the sink, but she was no match for Maria's aim. Cottage cheese dripped down her fringe and her face, down her jumper and on to the floor. Maria was laughing so much she missed her next aim. The cheese slid in white globs down the kitchen window, landing in a pile on the sill. "It looks like bird poo!" giggled Emily, wiping her face with her jumper. Both girls watched the cottage cheese and laughed till they cried. Then Emily reached behind her and filled a jug with water from the tap.

"You wouldn't dare!" warned Maria, as Emily stood there, threatening her with it. "If you throw it, you'll have to clear it up!"

"You can," retorted Emily. "You started it." She grinned, took careful aim and the cold water arced across the kitchen and caught Maria's front, making her gasp. Emily whooped with laughter.

Fun though it might be, Maria did not intend to lose this battle. "Pay back time," she said through gritted teeth, eyes glinting. She snatched the butter dish off the worktop, scooped the butter into her hand and advanced towards Emily.

"Don't!" yelled Emily through her laughter. "No! That's all the butter we've got left!" She ducked down and made a dash for the back door, but Maria was too quick. She caught her and smeared the butter into Emily's hair and over her face, then wiped the last traces on the sleeve of her jumper. Emily struggled and screamed, trying to pull herself away, but the combination of cottage cheese, ham and water on the floor made a lethal combination. She slipped, pulling Maria down with her. They both lay there on the floor until their laughter subsided, then Maria took a look at the kitchen. What a mess! Her jumper was soaked at the front, but she noted with satisfaction that Emily had come off by far the worst. Butter, cottage cheese and pieces of ham were stuck all over her.

"You'd better have a shower," she suggested calmly, getting up. "You look a state. Then you'd better clear up this lot before Mum and Dad come back. They'll have a fit, seeing the mess you made."

"I made!" retorted Emily. "You started it! And you made more mess than me. You can help!" But Emily's indignant plea fell on deaf ears and Maria went up to her room to change, smiling in satisfaction.

"I won't do it!" Emily called after her, but Maria didn't believe her. Mummy's pet would have to clear it up all on her own. What a shame!

Emily was nowhere to be seen when Maria came down later for a belated lunch. The kitchen was clean though, Maria noted to her satisfaction. She poured herself a large coke, took several slices of bread spread thickly with honey into the lounge and ate it curled up in the reclining armchair, which was strictly forbidden. "The dining room is for dining" was one of Dad's favourite sayings. She made plenty of noise so Emily would know that she was there, but it didn't work. Emily didn't come out of hiding all afternoon.

This meant that there was little to distract Maria from her increasingly worried thoughts and nobody to take out her frustration on. The land phone was still dead and she still had no signal on her mobile. The battery was running low, too, which was worrying, as there was no way of recharging it. She looked through some old magazines, but found it difficult to concentrate. Why were Mum and Dad taking so long? Something must have gone wrong. But what? Maybe Granny or Grandpa had been taken ill and they had had to go to hospital. Or maybe the car had broken down. Maria had other, darker ideas, but she pushed them away without giving them space.

The hours crept by slowly and light gave way to darkness, which covered everything with cold, hard shadows. The dark furniture began to look grim and forbidding. Maria considered lighting some candles, but last night's experience put her off. She went round the house, checking that all the outside doors and windows were locked. At least by daylight everything had seemed normal – you could pretend. Now things started to take on a more sinister perspective. The darkness seemed to be enjoying stealing up on her, playing with her fears, like a cat with a mouse, waiting to pounce on her when she wasn't looking. Maria shivered as she started to pace up and down the long, grey hallway. Every little noise and movement made her jump. She was fast becoming more frightened than she had ever been in her life. Her stomach started to churn and she could feel her heart beating hard in her chest. She became angry too; what right did anyone have to treat her like this? She was angry with the planes, angry with the government for not stopping them. Angry with her parents for leaving her like this – how dare they? Angry with Emily for being her parents' favourite and angry because she feared spending the dark night alone.

To stop the rising tide of panic, Maria took a grip on herself and began to draw up a plan of action. She and Emily would cycle to Granny and Grandpa's – find out what was going on. True, Mum had told them to wait at home, but something was obviously wrong. They couldn't go now – they would leave first thing in the morning. The adults would probably be back by then, Maria told herself, but they ought to be prepared, just in case . . . The first thing was to check the bikes – they hadn't been used for a while. She was glad the garage was attached to the kitchen. There was no way she was going outside in the dark.

Both bikes looked fine, as far as Maria could see. Bit dusty, but the tyres weren't flat. She found a decent torch in the garage and began to feel a bit better. The next thing was to find suitable food. Maria searched through the dark kitchen cupboards; to the items she had put in her backpack last night she added two packets of chocolate biscuits and four cans of coke. They shouldn't need anything really – they should easily be back by lunchtime, but it was just as well to be prepared. Mum and Dad had only intended to be a couple of hours . . . The thought of what they would do if they got to her grandparents' house and back without finding anyone, Maria refused to entertain. But they couldn't stay here for ever, just waiting.

She wrote a short note to her parents, then went to Emily's room to inform her sister of her plan. It didn't go down very well.

five

The next day dawned cold and drizzly, which matched Maria's mood perfectly. Fortunately, by the time the girls left the house after a hurried coffee, the rain had stopped, although there was still a damp chill in the air. Maria hesitated as she placed the note for her parents on the bureau in the hall. She could hardly believe that they were really leaving. But the bang as she closed the front door had an air of finality about it. For better or worse, they had left.

Maria had expected Emily to be difficult about going, but she had just got ready quietly. She had seemed too tired to argue. Two bad nights were taking their toll. Last night, by mutual agreement, the girls had brought their duvets down and slept in the lounge; after a shared supper of tomato soup and the last of the bread, both were reluctant to be on their own in the cold and dark again. Emily had offered to have the two-seater settee as she was shorter; Maria had agreed and taken the larger one, but she had still slept badly. All night long, in and out of sleep, she had hoped to hear a key in the lock or a familiar voice, but neither had happened. If the circumstances had been different – if she had been with her friends rather than a pathetic little sister and if there had been no planes dropping bombs, brooded Maria, this might have been fun.

Neither of the girls spoke as they took the road towards Sonbridge – both were wrapped up in their own tired thoughts, with very little traffic to disturb them, considering it was supposed to be rush hour. Maria felt uneasy. She had made this plan out of desperation. Now that they were carrying it out she wondered if it was a good idea. Pink blossom on the trees waved cheerily in the breeze and fluffy white clouds chased the rain clouds away, but Maria felt dull and heavy.

They crossed the bridge over the M25. "Look at those people down there!" called Emily from behind. "There are people cycling on the motorway! And walking – look! They're not allowed to do that – they'll get caught by the police!"

Maria stopped in the middle of the bridge and Emily drew up alongside. They looked down. Maria felt tense, anxious. There was traffic, but it wasn't normal traffic. There were usually loads of lorries thundering along; now there were hardly any, but plenty of cars and vans laden with people and possessions fled past beneath them, some pulling trailers and caravans. One supermarket lorry had overturned on the hard shoulder and several cars had been abandoned. Maybe they had run out of petrol, thought Maria. Mum had said that it might be difficult to get. And as Emily had noticed, there was what looked like a family cycling along and several groups of pedestrians walking along the grass verges, weighed down with heavy packs and bags. "Maybe the police aren't going to work," she thought aloud. That was a frightening thought. That meant that anyone could do anything. Steal, rape, murder – and get away with it. And people seemed to be on the move. A chill went down her spine. It was dangerous out here; anything could happen. Maybe they should have stayed at home. For a minute Maria contemplated turning back, but then she remembered the cold, empty home they had left – they had to find their parents. She steeled herself. They would go on.

Taking a deep breath, Maria set off, Emily following. Maria blamed herself for not listening to the news yesterday – she ought to have found out what was going on. Dad's Mercedes was still in the garage, she should have listened to the radio in that, like Dad had done. For the first time in her life, Maria felt responsible for her actions. Not only for herself, but for Emily too. It was so unfair, brooded Maria; two days ago the most important decision she needed to make was what to wear to Trudi's birthday party. Now the decisions she was being forced to make could mean life or death, literally.

It was still early when the girls reached the outskirts of the town. To start with, apart from an eerie stillness, everything looked very much the same as it always had. The grey stone tower of the parish church stood tall and proud, pretending to look indestructible, although Maria knew better. But where were the people? The usual rows of houses, offices and pubs still lined the empty streets, although as they got closer to the main shopping area, more and more of them were damaged – glass smashed, window boxes overturned, signs twisted. Maria's stomach churned. It was like a ghost town. As they entered the High Street she stopped, unprepared for the shock. Emily rode up next to her. "Look at the shops," she said in a scared voice.

"What do you think I'm doing, Stupid?" Every single glass front had been smashed – shops, travel agents, pubs, cafés, estate agents – none had escaped the violence. Pedestrian lights, litter bins, bus shelters, shop signs – all had been vandalised. Glass and rubbish littered the road and pavement. A small group of elderly women with shopping bags were talking in front of what used to be a supermarket, looking in at the damage; apart from them, the street was completely deserted. It was barely recognisable; it looked more like something you would see on the news, far away, in a country where there had been some catastrophe.

Maria set off again in shocked disbelief, dodging the rubbish, glass and twisted metal with difficulty. Emily followed. "Do you think those people are hungry?" She anxiously indicated the group of ladies, who stared at them as they passed. Maria just shrugged. She wanted to be left alone with her thoughts. Slowing down, she peered through what was left of the supermarket doors. It was just an empty wreck. A pile of magazines and other goods lay in spoiled heaps, but everything of any value seemed to have disappeared. All the shops were the same. The gangs that Dad had mentioned, destroying and looting. They must have come here to Sonbridge, of all places! The enormity of it all was too difficult to take in. Maria wondered what people were going to do for food until it could all be rebuilt. It would take weeks. Thank goodness there was always a full larder at the cottage.

At the next crossroads, Maria turned left. Emily nearly shot past, taken by surprise. Maria waited for her to catch up.

"Where are we going?" demanded Emily. "I thought we were going to Granny and Grandpa's?"

"We'll try the surgery first, it's nearer."

"Why? Do you think Mum and Dad might be there?"

Maria couldn't think of a polite reply, so she didn't bother. Now they were nearing their destination, she was starting to feel really afraid. And furious for being left in charge of Emily. It wasn't fair. If something happened to her, she would get the blame. And suppose they found something awful? Maria held her breath as they swept round a sharp bend to the surgery. "Come on," said Maria roughly, hurrying Emily through the gate, then she stopped. Like the shops in the High Street, the surgery had been badly damaged and appeared abandoned. Most of the windows had been smashed, two young trees had been snapped off and through the broken glass the girls could see the reception area looking like a film set after a violent movie – computers smashed, files in muddled heaps, desks overturned and seats slashed.

"Oh no!" breathed Emily. "I don't think Mum and Dad are here." Emily had obviously not realised how serious it was, thought Maria. She felt like hitting her for being so stupid, but she kept her mouth shut and her hands to herself. The girls left their bikes by the front door. Maria hesitated. "Wait here," she told her.

"No way! I'm coming in too."

"I said, 'Wait here'!" said Maria savagely. She pushed Emily into the waiting room. "Don't move!" she warned her. Maria dreaded what she might find. She couldn't risk letting Emily see anything awful.

"Don't leave me!" wailed Emily.

"Shut up, I'll only be a minute." Maria paused and took a deep breath. She went up the corridor, looking in all the doctors' rooms, glass crunching under the soles of her shoes. Each one showed the same story. Cupboards ripped off the walls, emptied of their contents, computers and equipment smashed, chairs mutilated.

"Have you found anything?" called Emily from the waiting room in a high-pitched voice.

"Not yet." Maria went quickly upstairs to the offices and gasped involuntarily as she entered the seminar room. There was nobody there now. But there had been. Blood spattered the cream walls. Chairs lay higgledy-piggledy round the room. And Mum's navy handbag lay on the floor next to a smashed overhead projector. The handle had been ripped off the bag and its contents were spilling out into a pool of congealing blood. Maria went hot and cold. She swallowed. Her legs shook and she grabbed the side of the door for support. Then she vomited.

"Maria, what's the matter?" screamed Emily.

six

It only took five minutes to cycle to Granny and Grandpa's house, but to Maria every minute seemed like an eternity. The vivid picture of the handbag and the blood haunted her, forcing her to go faster, faster along the near-deserted roads. She felt like she was going to burst. It was hard work, struggling uphill, but all Maria could think of was getting to the house. The girls didn't speak. Serve Emily right if she was crying, thought Maria savagely. She'd told her to stay downstairs. Maria squeezed her eyes to check her own tears. Was it Mum's blood? Images of her mother's mutilated body came uninvited to Maria's mind, but she pushed them fiercely away and cycled even faster. No, no, no! But if it wasn't Mum's blood, whose was it? And where were Mum and Dad now? They had to be at Granny's! They just had to be!

"Please slow down, Maria," wailed Emily tearfully, getting left further and further behind. Maria slowed a little, but not enough to let Emily catch up. She didn't want to go slower, even though her legs were aching and her breath was coming in gasps. And anyway, she was glad that Emily was getting left behind. Serve her right for being such a pain, she thought. It was her own stupid fault she'd seen Mum's handbag. And the blood.

At last Maria reached The Crescent. The curving rows of solid, red brick Victorian houses in the leafy lane still had the genteel air of a bygone era. Maria was surprised that nothing looked vandalised here; it seemed almost odd to see something normal now. She skidded to a halt outside number 16, chucked her bike and backpack in the bushes and took the few steps to the green front door in a flying leap. Then she hesitated, gasping for breath. She still felt queasy from the shock at the surgery and her arms and legs ached. She tried to stop shaking, but she couldn't. She was sweating, though she felt cold and her heart was thumping loudly. She was also vaguely aware that she was very thirsty. And too scared to knock on the door. She watched Emily cycle up to the gate, panting noisily, face pale and tear-stained, hair in a tangled mess. "You could have waited," wailed Emily between gasps. "It's not my fault I can't cycle as fast as you!" Maria ignored her. Emily collapsed on to the doorstep. "Have you knocked?" she asked anxiously.

Maria looked at her sister scathingly, although inside she felt like a nervous wreck. "I was waiting for you," she mocked, then, taking a deep breath, Maria rapped boldly on the brass knocker, shattering the silent emptiness. She could feel her heart beating fast in her chest. She looked round and listened, fearfully. Nothing, nobody. No one greeted them at the door or waved to them from the windows. The only sign of life was the innocent fluttering of the spring flowers and shrubs in the garden. Maria felt like screaming. She knocked again, this time louder, then, leaving every pretence at cool assurance behind, banged on the door and shouted, "Open the door!"

It made no difference. There was no one there to answer it. "They must be dead," Emily wailed, clutching her head in her hands. "They're all dead and we're the only ones left!"

Maria ran wildly round the side of the house in desperate hope – maybe everyone was round the back! Maybe they hadn't heard the door . . . Emily followed, choking back loud sobs. But Mum's car wasn't in the drive, Grandpa wasn't pottering in the garden. There was no smell of dinner cooking, no Radio 4, no clattering of pots. All the windows were closed, all the curtains were still. They were on their own. No! Maria had gone over this scene in her mind a thousand times during the night; it didn't end like this! Granny was supposed to open the door and give her a hug; they would all say how brilliantly she had coped, then everyone would go home together . . .

Desperately, Maria tried the back door. To her surprise, it opened. She stood there, struggling with the shock. Why would anyone leave the back door unlocked, if they weren't at home? She called out hesitantly, "Granny?" Nothing. "Grandpa?" She fearfully, gingerly, pushed the door open and surveyed the familiar scene. The ancient red-topped kitchen table and the pine dresser stood in their usual places. And there was the rocking chair with the patchwork cushion, where Granny would sit and hum while she waited for the vegetables to cook. Or "used to", flashed through Maria's mind. She swallowed hard. Go in, or not? It was the surgery all over again.

"They're not there, they're dead," wailed Emily from behind. Her sobs spurred Maria on. "Shut up, Stupid," she hissed fiercely. They couldn't be dead. She took a deep breath and stepped in. Kitchen: empty. Dining room, sitting room, study: empty. Maria leapt up the stairs without daring to pause to think. Bedrooms and bathroom – all empty. She stood on the landing, wild with conflicting emotions. Now what?

Emily came running out of the main bedroom, flourishing an old-fashioned alarm clock. "Granny and Grandpa aren't dead," she announced, looking slightly dazed. "They've packed and gone away! The suitcases aren't on the wardrobe, and their toothbrushes and stuff have gone from the bathroom." Maria stared at Emily, hardly daring to believe it. "They went today!" continued Emily, waving the clock about, her voice trembling with emotion. "Grandpa wound up his clock this morning!"

"All right, Clever Clogs, maybe . . ." snapped Maria, then the two of them froze. Footsteps downstairs; someone must have seen their bikes!

"Coo-ee!" called a familiar voice. "Anybody there?" Maria breathed a sigh of relief and ran downstairs. It was old Mrs Fitchett from next door.

"Maria? Emily!" exclaimed Mrs Fitchett. "What are you doing here?" Maria ignored the question.

"Mrs Fitchett, where are Granny and Grandpa?" she asked urgently.

"Are they OK?" added Emily.

Mrs Fitchett looked rather taken aback. "They are absolutely fine! Your mother and father came to fetch them a little while ago." She waved a bony finger in their direction. "They said that you two were at home on your own! They didn't know you were out, gallivanting about on your bikes!" She peered over her glasses at them severely. "You had better get back home sharpish, or if I know your father . . ."

"What about Mum?" interrupted Maria anxiously.

The old lady stood there, looking rather bemused. "What do you mean, dear?"

Maria fumbled for the words. "She didn't look . . . well, injured?"

"We thought she might be dead or something," admitted Emily.

"Dead?" asked Mrs Fitchett, sounding astonished. "Of course she's not dead, I saw her not an hour ago with my own eyes." She shook her head and wagged her finger again. "All this fuss over a few bombs," she tutted. "In my day . . ."

"They're OK!" laughed Emily. "Oh, Maria, I really thought . . ." but she didn't finish her sentence, she just carried on laughing.

Waves of relief swept over Maria, immense relief and she whooped out loud. Everyone was alive and well! She ran to the front door. "Let's go!" she yelled. She felt she had been stretched to snapping point, like a length of elastic pulled until it would stretch no further, but now someone had let the ends go and she was free! All they had to do now was go home. She laughed aloud again, unable to stop herself. "Thank you, Mrs Fitchett!" she called back as she ran down the path to her bike. "You're my best friend!"

Mrs Fitchett shook her head and raised her eyebrows, although she did look pleased at the compliment. "You two sound like a pair of laughing hyenas!" she called. "You'd better calm down and mind how you go or you'll have an accident!"

"Don't worry!" called back Emily. "We'll be fine!"

At the corner of the road Maria stopped, remembering her thirst. She slung her backpack round and fished out two cans of coke, one of which she passed to her sister. Both gulped gratefully. "Thanks," said Emily. "I didn't know you'd brought drinks."

"What did you think I had in my bag, Stupid?" sneered Maria. "The kitchen sink?"

seven

It was a while before the girls spoke again. Emily's probably thinking, "Told you so," thought Maria. Well, maybe they should have stayed at home, but how was she supposed to know that everyone was on their way back? And Emily had been right about the suitcases and the clock; that was pretty impressive, although extremely irritating. Maria sighed inwardly. And now she would get a load of mouth from Dad – oh well, that was normal!

Without too much difficulty, Maria shook herself free of all her negative thoughts and gave a great whoop of glee. Being in trouble was nothing new and at least everyone was alive. "Yee-ha!" she yelled as she swooped down the hill she had climbed so full of fear just a few minutes earlier. She began to sing Slash's latest number one hit at the top of her voice:

We've got release and we're gonna be free,
Yeah, yeah, we're gonna be free!
Give us what we need and we're gonna be free,
Yeah, yeah, we're gonna be free!

Emily joined in and they both yelled the song joyfully at

the tops of their voices, ignoring the few people and the handful of cars that passed them. At last Maria started to feel free. Free from the fear, free from the tension, free from the responsibility that had lain so heavily. In a little while they would all be on their way to the cottage together! Yes!

But as the jubilation began to pass, Maria fell to wondering how they had managed to miss Mum's car. That was unbelievably frustrating. She must have driven round the back way because of the state of the High Street. And how had her handbag ended up in the seminar room at Dad's surgery? Stolen, maybe. The blood was a total mystery. It was strange, too, that Mum and Dad only turned up at Granny and Grandpa's a little while ago; so where did they spend last night? Maria shrugged it off. Maybe Mrs Fitchett was mistaken. Then something else crossed her mind. "Why do you think Granny and Grandpa left their back door unlocked?" she called back to Emily.

"Granny's mother always left their back door open when Granny was little," replied Emily, "in World War II. Then if anyone's house was bombed they'd have somewhere to go. I bet Granny thought she'd do that too."

"Yeah," agreed Maria. That would be just like Granny, to leave the door open for anyone in trouble. She grinned at Emily. "Dad would say, 'That's a risky thing to do.'" She imitated Dad at his most pompous and Emily laughed agreement. Dad was *so* boring! But Granny was different. She always seemed to do the right thing, somehow, even if it wasn't what you'd expect. She and Grandpa were fun, always full of treats and surprises. Maria's thoughts turned affectionately to her Granny and Grandpa for a minute, but that opened up a flood of emotions, so with determination she pushed reality away. She made up a beautiful dream instead, of strolling along a sun-kissed, palm-fringed beach with Adam Johanssen. They would walk hand in hand along the soft, golden sand, watching the sunset, listening to the gentle waves lapping at their feet.

"Excuse me . . ." A male voice calling brought Maria back to the present. A tall, handsome black lad of about her own age was running over to them from the other side of the road, dressed in a dark suit and white shirt with a navy and yellow striped tie.

Maria and Emily stopped, warily. "I'm aiming for Dover. Am I going in the right direction?" asked the lad, with a wide, incredibly friendly smile.

"Dover?" repeated Maria cautiously, questioning whether she had heard right. He didn't seem to have a car.

"Yes," he assured her. "I need to get a ferry to France."

"You can't walk there!" said Maria, rather scathingly. Their cottage wasn't far from Dover – it took a couple of hours to drive there! She raised her eyebrows at Emily which meant, "We've got a weird one here!"

"You may think I'm crazy," grinned the lad, totally unfazed. "But where I come from it's quite normal for people to walk long distances if there isn't any transport."

"Do you go to Sonbridge School?" asked Emily, changing the subject.

"You recognised the tie!" he replied cheerfully. "Arthur Lamba," he introduced himself politely, holding out his hand for the girls to shake. Maria found herself warming to him, odd though he was. She couldn't help smiling back; his grin was just amazing.

"Maria Reynolds," she said in return. "And this is Emily. My sister."

"I'm delighted to meet you," he continued, still smiling, "but what I really need is directions to Dover. I am heading in the right direction, aren't I?"

Maria thought about it. Her geography of Kent was a bit hazy. She tried to think of the route to Callum. "I think you need to head for Cartford," she replied eventually. "Normally you'd go on the M20, but I don't suppose you want to walk on the motorway?" Arthur laughed and slapped his thigh as if Maria had made a funny joke.

"People are walking on the M25; we've seen them," interjected Emily.

He smiled cheerfully. "Well, I'll not follow their example!"

"Then I think the best way would be . . . left at the next crossroads." Maria indicated a junction a little further on. "You go through Parrin Green, it's the next village – then you just follow the signs for Cartford, I think . . . though I don't really know," she added doubtfully. Trudi lived at Parrin Green. What did the signposts say? She had seen them often enough! "Yes, aim for Cartford," she repeated. She realised how vague she was sounding. Her brain ached and she was finding it difficult to think straight. Well, if it was wrong, it was just tough. She prepared to set off again.

"Parrin Green, Cartford!" repeated Arthur. "Thank you

so much! I was just praying that God would help me find the way!" And he waved cheerily to the girls as they left.

Maria cringed. "Total freak!" she decided out loud. Religion was OK for old people, but it was embarrassing coming from someone her own age.

"At least he was friendly," argued Emily.

Maria didn't reply. He was OK, except for the God bit. Pity really, otherwise he was quite fanciable! Handsome, certainly and she'd never been out with a black guy. But he wasn't like Adam . . . Maria sighed, forgot Arthur and returned to sipping cocktails in her tropical paradise.

There was virtually no traffic now, even on the motorway, but Maria hardly noticed, let alone cared. It was no longer her responsibility – they would be home soon! But as the girls cycled on, relief turned to an overwhelming tiredness that seemed to blot everything else out. Why doesn't Mum come and get us, Maria thought crossly, as she struggled to keep turning the pedals. She hadn't got a broken leg and she must have found their note ages ago. A bang in the distance interrupted her thoughts.

"Stop!" hissed Emily, sounding scared. "What's that noise?"

"For goodness sake, Chicken," said Maria impatiently, "it's not a gun! It's just a car door closing, for goodness sake!" Then her tired brain caught up with her. It must be Mum's car. There weren't any other houses or cars to go in them for miles; Mr Kingsley-Brown had left ages ago. Relief and joy that someone was at home were mixed with annoyance that nobody had bothered to come and fetch them before, but Maria put on a spurt of energy. "It's Mum's car, Idiot! They're packing the cars up!" Emily caught on.

"They're at home!" she yelled in delight. "Yes, yes, yes!"

In a minute they would be home themselves – Maria could already see the red-brick chimneys through the trees. Her thoughts turned to collapsing into a comfortable chair and being brought lunch. Two more bends in the road and luxury was within reach! Another car roared to life in the distance and there was the faint scrunch of pebbles in the drive. That must be Grandpa in Dad's Mercedes!

"They're all coming to find us!" yelled Emily excitedly, hearing the two cars pull out of the drive.

"Yee-ha!" whooped Maria. "Grandpa to the rescue!" But a split second later she realised that the sound of the cars' engines wasn't coming nearer, it was getting further away. A wave of fear chilled her to the core. "No, no!" she begged under her breath, cycling a little faster. Why were they going the other way? If they weren't careful, they would miss them . . . maybe she had heard wrong . . .

"They're going the other way!" screeched Emily, sounding as desperate as Maria felt. "They're leaving without us!"

Maria could hardly think. This couldn't be happening. "Shout!" she screamed. They turned the last bend, shouting, screaming and waving, but the two familiar cars just drove on. The girls stopped at the end of the drive and stared at the fast-receding cars. "I don't believe it!" said Maria, stunned.

"They didn't see us!" whispered Emily. "Maybe they've

gone to look for us another way . . ."

"There is no other way to Granny and Grandpa's, Stupid! Can't you see? They've gone to the cottage. Without us."

eight

"We can catch them up!" shouted Emily desperately. "Maria, come on!" Emily set off helter-skelter down the road in pursuit of the cars. Maria didn't know whether to laugh or cry or scream. She knew it was useless. They could never catch up now. Fury was taking over from disbelief. "They hate us, that's why they left us!" she shouted at the top of her voice, hurling her bike down in anger. Tears of rage started to fall involuntarily down her cheeks and she gave her bike a rough kick, then stopped herself doing it again. She might need it. She stormed up the drive to the house and threw her backpack ferociously into the porch while she fumbled with her key.

The house was still and empty. "Mum, Dad!" screamed Maria, though she knew they weren't there to hear her. "I hate you!" Then she stopped. Why was everything in such a mess? Weird. Surely Mum and Dad wouldn't have chucked the contents of the bureau on the floor? And why had they taken the pictures from the walls? Puzzled, Maria went in to the study. The computer was gone, so were Mum's golfing trophies and all the silver from the cabinet. No doubt Mum and Dad were planning on selling their valuable stuff for cash, in case the banks weren't open.

Surely not the computer though? And why were all the filing cabinet drawers open and a vase of flowers tipped over on the windowsill? They must have been in such a blind panic – what idiots, Maria thought scornfully. In her anger she thumped the door viciously on her way out.

She went to the lounge – it was the same scenario, an utter mess, everything of value gone. Then Maria stood, stock-still. The patio doors had been smashed. Shattered fragments of glass littered the rug, jagged edges clung to the door frames and a slight breeze through the gash made the red velvet curtains shudder forlornly. Someone had forced an entry. They had been burgled.

Maria ran in a panic up to her own room. Her birthday telly! She stood in horrified disbelief in the doorway. Her room never looked neat exactly, but at least it was usually her own mess. Now the contents of her drawers and wardrobe lay in ravaged heaps, even her underwear and make-up, chucked all over the place by strangers. Her telly had gone along with all her other electrical items; dustless rectangles on the furniture showed where they had stood. Maria felt ill. Sick people had taken her things and been through her private possessions. Then a chilling thought filled her – what would have happened if she and Emily had been here when the burglars had come? A worse thought sent a shiver of fear down her spine. What if they were still in the house now? She whirled round in a panic, to check behind her. No, of course they couldn't be. Her parents had been here since then. She walked slowly back downstairs, a heavy ache groaning in the depths of her being. She had been violated by strangers and abandoned by her family. How much more could a person take?

Emily ran in through the open front doorway, panting. "They didn't wait!" she wailed, almost beside herself. "Why didn't they wait?" She stopped in her tracks when she noticed the state of the hall. "What . . .?" she began, but ran out of words.

Maria sat on the bottom stair, head in her hands. What were they going to do now? Why hadn't their parents tidied up a bit and made the house secure before they left? And why hadn't they come to look for her and Emily, or at least waited until they got back? Mum and Dad may have been cross with them for not staying at home, but surely, surely they wouldn't have deliberately gone without them? Then she twigged. With Emily watching in open-mouthed disbelief, Maria got on her hands and knees and rifled through the papers on the floor by the bureau. In amongst the bills and brown envelopes was her note. Nobody had seen it.

Maria went into the lounge, pushed the best reclining armchair back against the wall from where she could watch both doors and collapsed into it. Emily ran in from the hall and hovered nervously by the chair. "I've found a letter," she announced, her voice shaking. "It's addressed to me and you. Shall I open it?" Maria reached up, snatched the envelope out of Emily's hand and tore it open. It was in Granny's handwriting.

My dearest Maria and Emily,

You can't know what a shock it was for us all to find that burglars have been here and you two lovely girls gone. We'll tell you all about why we weren't here yesterday when we see you. Your Mum and Dad have been beside themselves with worry. But knowing how sensible you are and seeing that you've taken your bikes, we hope you're already on your way to the cottage. We're going to set out any minute ourselves, hoping to catch up with you as quickly as we can, but I thought I'd just write you a quick note to let you know what we're doing, just in case, you never know. Grandpa and I are taking your Dad's car, so there will be plenty of room for all of us if we meet you on the way, but if we don't, I promise you that we will keep looking for you until we find you.

I must finish because everyone is ready to go, but I just want to say that we all send lots of love and we entrust you to our dear friend Jesus. I know our loving heavenly Father will look after you. We have asked him to send angels to guard you. So we look forward to seeing you soon. God bless you both, my dears.

With all our love,

Granny

xxxxxx

Maria held out the note to Emily, who had been waiting anxiously next to her, then she sank deep into the chair. Her mind was a whirl. At least they hadn't been deliberately abandoned, but her tired mind and emotions were struggling with the enormity of their predicament. They had been left behind.

"Burglars!" whispered Emily, wide-eyed, as she read. Then she let out a cry of horror. "They think we've gone to the cottage!" She looked round in fear. "What are we going to do?"

Maria felt like letting rip, because she didn't know. She just wanted to be left on her own for a while to think things through. But she couldn't face another row, or any more tears. She'd have to be nice to Emily. She grimaced. "At least we weren't here when the burglars came. Let's make some lunch and think about it, shall we? It's a bit early, but it doesn't matter."

Emily nodded. She looked even paler than usual and very close to tears. "I'll make it if you like."

"OK," said Maria distantly, feeling very fragile herself. "I don't know what we've got . . ."

"Anything will do." Just go, she thought.

Emily went.

Maria closed her eyes.

nine

By the time Emily came back with lunch, Maria was poring over a road map. She had made a list of things they would need for the journey: food, drinks, spare clothes, sleeping bags, towels, toiletries, torches, bike lights. She tried all the phones again, including her mobile, to no avail and even searched for her old one, but it had been stolen, along with everything else. When everything got back to normal, Maria thought grimly to herself, she would have one big insurance claim to make!

Despite a deep tiredness, she was starting to feel more positive. She and Emily would cycle to the cottage. However overwhelming the thought, they had to get away from this house and if that Arthur boy could walk to Dover, they could cycle to Callum. They would have to take food with them as there might not be any shops open, and they would have to find somewhere to stay, hopefully for only one night, but they would cross that bridge when they came to it. Perhaps there would be a youth hostel or bed and breakfast somewhere.

Maria noticed from the map that she'd given Arthur good directions. Like him, they would avoid the motorway; it could be dangerous and anyway, the country roads actually looked like a more direct route, cut out a big corner. Mind you, it was still a long way, a very long way, reflected Maria as she traced the roads with her finger on the map. But no doubt Mum or Grandpa would find them before they'd gone far . . .

Maria looked up as Emily held out a plate to her. The half-smile she had intended for her sister froze on her lips. "What's the matter?" she asked rather shortly. Emily's face was white and drawn, apart from her eyes, which were red and puffy where she had been crying. She silently handed Maria a plate with a split bagel, inexpertly spread with red jam.

"Where's the butter?" Maria demanded testily. "And you're supposed to toast bagels. Don't tell me it's taken you all this time to spread two of these with a bit of jam?"

Emily wiped her eyes with the back of her shaking hand. "I found the bagels in the freezer. I had to wait for them to finish defrosting before I could cut them." She sounded scared. "I couldn't find anything else."

"What do you mean, you couldn't find anything else?"

"There isn't much left," stammered Emily. "The burglars have taken all the food. And all my things from my bedroom."

Maria looked up in exasperation. "The food?" she repeated. "Don't be stupid, burglars don't steal food! If the food's gone, Mum and Dad must have taken it!"

Maria got up and marched out to the kitchen, scattering the road atlas, pen and paper as she went. This information was a big blow. Never mind Emily's rubbish; food was at the top of her list. For once, Emily didn't follow. Maria opened all the food cupboards, fridge and freezer, one by one. Emily was right. The only edibles remaining were a few wrinkled potatoes and the dregs of a pot of jam. Someone had taken it all; tins, packets, fruit, vegetables and the entire contents of the fridge and freezer. "Thanks very much," Maria muttered savagely under her breath.

As she spoke, a cloud passed over the sun and a dark chill touched the room. Maria shuddered involuntarily. She suddenly felt very lonely. And very, very tired. She fought with the temptation to go to bed, pull her duvet over her head and forget everything. But suppose the burglars came back? Anyway, she didn't want to face her room again right now. Tight-lipped, she returned to her seat in the lounge, tore the two pages they would need out of the road atlas and picked up her plate in silence.

"You can have my lunch," offered Emily generously. "I'm not hungry."

"Eat it!" ordered Maria.

"Honestly, I don't feel . . ." began Emily, but Maria cut her short.

"Eat it! It might be the last food you see for a long time."

Emily looked at the bagel, trying to keep her face from crumpling. "You don't really think Mum and Dad meant to leave us here, do you?" she asked.

"No," said Maria sharply.

"They will come back and get us, won't they?"

Maria paused a minute before answering, struggling not only with trying to be nice to Emily, but at having to say aloud something that she was hardly ready to accept herself yet. "Look, Em," she managed, hating Emily's tear-stained face, her straggly hair and her stupid brace, but above all, hating what she was forcing herself to say. "They didn't see our note. It was on the floor with the stuff the burglars chucked about. Remember? You saw me pick it up?" Emily nodded, comprehension and despair written all over her face. Maria took a deep breath. "Nobody meant to leave us here, they thought we'd already gone to the cottage. That's why they were in such a hurry, to catch up with us. When they get there and discover we're not there, they'll come and find us – Granny says so in the note. That's assuming they've got any petrol left. But even if they do, we can't wait here; it's not safe." She indicated the broken French window. "Whoever did that might come back. Or someone else might."

Emily sniffed and looked at the broken glass. "What are we going to do then?"

"We're going to cycle to the cottage. We'll eat, then pack."

Emily stared at her in disbelief. "We can't do that!"

"Mum and Dad think we can; they think we have!"

"But it's much too far – and it will be dark!"

"Look, Em, we've got to think positive," said Maria firmly. "We can just stay here, moan and cry until we die of starvation or someone comes and kills us, or we can cycle to the cottage. Get it?" Maria had intended to make the last bit sound light-hearted, but actually it came out rather sarcastically.

Emily's eyes were swimming again. "Couldn't we stay

at Granny and Grandpa's house? Mrs Fitchett could look after us."

"Mrs Fitchett?" repeated Maria hotly. "There's absolutely no way Mrs Fitchett's ever going to look after me! I'd rather starve! Look, I'm really tired and I've got a headache coming on. I don't feel like arguing, so just eat your bagel. When you're ready, come and give me a hand to pack the stuff we need, OK?"

Maria stalked out with her bagel without waiting for a reply and slammed the door hard, then wished she hadn't. That hurt her head. She had meant to be kind, but Emily did get up her nose – Mrs Fitchett indeed! What a pathetic suggestion! Stupid girl! Maria searched for some headache tablets in the kitchen, but the first aid box had gone too. Typical, she thought. Now I've got a throbbing headache. That made her think of Dad. No wonder he gets headaches, with me having a go at him all the time, she sighed to herself, gripping the edge of the sink and staring out at the neat back garden. Maybe he was thinking, "At last, free of Maria!" An unexpected wave of tenderness swept over her, a longing for her parents which made her throat ache and her eyes sting and she wished she hadn't been so horrible to them. She blinked back the tears. "Sorry," she mouthed silently to no one in particular, although the garden seemed to forgive her. It looked peaceful outside in the gentle sunlight. The neat lawn, the circular rose bed, the borders of green shrubs and nodding spring flowers, the orchard of apple trees laden with white blossom and the misty hills beyond – she used to complain about how boring it all was, but at least it was familiar. She didn't want to leave. She didn't want it to be like this. Then she wondered if Emily was right. Maybe the thieves had taken the food – after all, food was precious right now. Maybe the others had nothing to eat either. The thought of them hungry hit her in the pit of her stomach. To stop herself thinking, Maria went in search of the panniers for the bikes.

Emily joined Maria as she began to make a pile of essentials in the hall. "Get one spare set of clothes, a towel, your toothbrush and your backpack," ordered Maria, ticking off her list.

"My suitcase has gone."

"So's mine. So what?"

"My clothes were in it."

"Then find some other clothes, Stupid! Don't tell me you packed them all!" But Emily still hung around nervously. "Well?" demanded Maria impatiently.

Emily hesitated. "How long do you think it will take us to get to the cottage?"

Maria forced herself to sound normal. "I reckon it'll take us a couple of days."

Emily's face dropped and she stared. "But it only takes two hours in the car!"

"Yeah, but that's on the motorway, doing 70 miles an hour. We won't be doing either of those. We could be there by tomorrow night if we get on with it." Maria thought about it for a minute. "Say Friday, just to be sure, because today's only half a day. But we'll stick to the main roads, then with a bit of luck Mum or Grandpa will find us and pick us up well before that."

"But where are we going to sleep? And what are we going to eat and drink?" Emily sounded mutinous.

"How do I know?" snapped Maria. Of all the people she could have been left with, it had to be Emily!

"The shops might not be open. And anyway, I haven't got any money, have you?"

"Not much," grimaced Maria, "but we'll manage. We'll just have to."

ten

To Maria's relief, when Emily came back downstairs with her spare clothes and a fluffy blue towel, she seemed calmer. She even managed an attempt at a smile. "It's like we're going camping for a weekend," she had said. Maria didn't trust herself to reply. As if she'd go camping with Emily! Maybe I could lose her on the way, Maria smirked to herself, knowing that she wouldn't dare – but the idea was tempting!

It took a while to get everything together. The girls stuffed their panniers and backpacks until they would hold no more. The sleeping bags were bulky and took up a lot of room, but it couldn't be helped; there was no way they could be left out.

Being busy had prevented Maria from considering the enormity of what they were about to do, but as she sat alone on her bike in the drive, waiting for Emily to get some last forgotten item, it hit her hard. Shadows were already beginning to lengthen across the driveway and a deep foreboding filled her. The tall trees and the wind seemed to be whispering together, plotting their malicious intentions high above, where she couldn't hear what they were saying. The evening chill seemed to be joining in the evil game, too; it was still only afternoon, but it was already stretching out its cold tentacles. Maria shivered and looked round in rising alarm at the creeping shadows, feeling small, alone and afraid. "Come on Emily," she muttered under her breath. It was the first time she could ever remember wanting to see her sister! Then she caught hold of herself and sat up straight. "You can't touch us!" Maria announced boldly to the sinister silence. "Granny and Grandpa are praying for us." At once she felt a peace that was almost tangible. It was like nothing she had ever felt before – like everything was going to be OK, like there was something, someone even, who was out there, taking care of them. Maria looked round, so strong was the feeling, but there was nothing to be seen. She laughed at herself for talking to nothing and checked that Emily had not seen her. But she was glad to feel more confident. The sick feeling in her stomach lessened and her headache felt a bit better, too.

The girls stopped at the end of the drive to take one last look at their house. It ought to have been a sad moment, but it was strangely meaningless. Maria felt flat, empty. She was leaving her home and it meant nothing. It was weird. The feeling worried her for a minute, but she pushed it away. At least she had survived. That had to be better than the people in London. Emily appeared to feel the same – she didn't say anything, but her face remained impassive. Maria gritted her teeth in determination. They would make it to the cottage – or at least as far as they needed to until they were picked up. It might not be easy, but they would do it! Maria wondered if Granny and

Grandpa were still praying. It felt like it.

The first part of Maria's plan was to visit Trudi at Parrin Green; it was lucky that they were headed that way anyway. Trudi's Mum would help them, give them something to eat, at least. Maria wanted reassurance and Trudi's mum was the perfect person. Not perfect in appearance, like her own mother, perfect as in sympathetic. Actually, Trudi's mum nearly always looked a mess. Her dyed blonde hair nearly always had dark roots showing and she didn't have the figure for tight trousers, but wore them anyway, which embarrassed Trudi no end. But she was always cheerful and friendly and nothing shocked her, which was just as well with Trudi for a daughter. Trudi was crazy. She was always having new piercings and tattoos and once she had had all her hair completely shaved off. But whenever Trudi's Mum found out about her daughter's "improvements" as she called them, she would just laugh and make everyone another cup of tea. Her stock reply to everything was, "As long as it's not drugs, I don't mind."

Dusk was falling by the time the girls reached Parrin Green. Maria fleetingly wondered if the lad they had met in town had made it this far yet; if he had been hoping to get some food, he would have been unlucky. The village green looked bare and empty, the little row of shops sat in darkness and there was not a soul to be seen anywhere.

Trudi's house, facing the green, looked as empty as the rest of the village. Nobody answered Maria's knock, nobody called out or spoke. The silence was eerie. Maria's heart beat a bit faster. Surely not everyone in the whole village could have left? The girls crossed the road to the green, anxious and confused, peering up at the dark, silent windows of the houses as they passed. There was no sign of life anywhere; only a flock of starlings swooping and squabbling in the trees in the gathering dusk. The peaceful confidence that Maria had felt when she had left home was vanishing fast – what did these villagers know that she did not? Even the dark clouds scudding overhead seemed to be getting away as fast as they could. Maria needed to think. Leaning her bike carefully against a tree, she sat on a bench and got out the remaining chocolate biscuits and the last two cans of coke.

"Where did you get those?" asked Emily, staring in surprise. "I thought we didn't have any food!"

"I took them to Granny's, but we didn't eat them. Make the most of it – it's all we've got left." The sound of the cans popping open sounded loud in the emptiness. It was a strange feeling, sitting on a park bench with the shadows lengthening, eating chocolate biscuits and sipping coke, homeless and alone.

"Why do you think there's nobody here?" asked Emily. Her voice sounded high and thin.

Maria shrugged. "How should I know?" But in her heart was a sinking feeling. Maybe everyone had been evacuated because more planes were coming back – maybe it would be worse this time. Maybe there would be a nuclear war or chemical weapons, maybe there would be tanks . . . Maria took out a handful of biscuits, stuffed the rest in her jacket pocket and got up to go. They had better get out of here as fast as they could. This was crazy! Last Saturday she had sat on this very bench with Trudi and Michelle, pigging sweets, laughing and messing about, while people walked their dogs and a bunch of little kids played football. It seemed like a very, very long time ago.

A sudden fast movement from the other side of the green made her whirl round. "There's a big dog coming!" cried Emily, gathering up her things in fright.

"Keep still!" warned Maria. She stood still herself, somewhat warily, but to the girls' relief the dog stopped a few metres away and lay down, panting and looking up at them. It was a rather thin, shaggy black-and-tan mongrel with a long muzzle and floppy ears. It put its head on one side, wagged its hairy tail and looked up at them with melting chocolate brown eyes.

"Woof!" it said, looking hopefully at Maria's biscuits. Maria's heart warmed to him. It looked as if he had been abandoned, like them. "Oh, he's so cute!" she crowed.

"He doesn't look as if he would bite, does he?" agreed Emily.

Maria stepped forward and held a biscuit out to him. "He's gorgeous! I bet he's hungry. He saw we'd got food." The dog crept forward. Maria smiled at him. She had always wanted a dog. Maybe she could keep this one! "Here, Doggie," she coaxed. He came forward, took the biscuit gently from her hand, swallowed it in one mouthful, then looked hopefully for more. "Please," his brown eyes seemed to plead. She held out another biscuit, but jumped back in alarm when the dog suddenly sprang up and started to bark madly. Emily, from behind, screamed. All in a flash, Maria realised that the dog was not barking at her, but at something behind. She gasped in horror as she turned.

eleven

"Emily!" screamed Maria, but she was too late. A dirty, unshaven old man in a shabby grey suit had made a lunge for Emily – or more precisely, Emily's biscuits – but she was holding so tightly onto them that he was pulling her away from the bench. His breath stank of alcohol and his clothes of grease and stale urine.

"Call your dog off me," snarled the man drunkenly, as the dog continued to bark menacingly at him.

"Let go my sister or I'll tell him to rip you apart!" shouted Maria, making no attempt to stop the dog.

The man was flustered and getting nasty. "Just give me the food," he snarled and put one hand round Emily's throat. She screamed and struggled, but held tightly to her biscuits.

Maria didn't hesitate. "Kill him!" she yelled and the dog jumped up and bit the man in his forearm, ripping the flesh with his teeth.

"Aagh!" shouted the man, letting go of Emily and staring in horror at his arm, which started to drip blood through the cuff of his filthy old shirt. "Evil dog!" he hissed. He aimed a kick at the dog and made a lunge for Emily as she tried to escape, but his co-ordination was poor and he missed the dog, missed his footing and tripped over the foot of the bench, landing on the ground with a heavy thud.

"Emily!" screamed Maria again. She tried to snatch her sister to safety as the man reached out to grab Emily's ankles, but she was too late.

"Got you!" snarled the man triumphantly as Emily fell.

"Help!" she screamed.

"I'm trying!" yelled Maria desperately, attempting to pull Emily from the man's grasp, but even with one wounded arm, his grip was strong.

"Give me the food!" demanded the man.

Maria kicked the man's hands, as hard as she could. "Never!" she screamed.

"You vicious little . . ." spat out the man, but he didn't finish his sentence. The dog bit his nearest leg and held on to the flesh with his teeth. "Aagh!" yelled the man again, releasing Emily and rolling round on the grass in pain, whacking out at the dog, who clung on, dodging the blows. Emily, still clutching her biscuits, scrambled to her feet.

Maria grabbed the bags. "Get on your bike!" she yelled at Emily. Shouting and gesturing wildly at the dog, the man bellowed drunkenly after the girls as they fled.

A little way up the road Maria stopped and turned, hoping to see the dog following them, but he was still holding the old man off. "Doggie, Doggie," she called, as soon as she had caught her breath, but he didn't come. Maria's heart was still pounding with the fright, but what surprised her was the depth of emotion she felt for her sister. For as long as she could remember, she had wished that something horrible would happen to Emily; now it had, she could hardly believe how terrified she had been and how glad she was that Emily was OK. "The man's not following," she panted. "You all right?" Emily nodded. She was clearly shaken, but not hurt.

"Maria, let's get out of here," she begged, her gaze fixed fearfully towards her assailant, who was shambling to his feet. "It's not safe!"

Maria agreed, but she tried to grin. "Well done for hanging on to the biscuits," she said. Emily tried to smile, but it was not a very successful attempt.

"Thanks for helping. That dog saved me. That man was so . . ." she ran out of words and burst in to tears.

"Forget that disgusting old tramp," said Maria firmly. "He's not worth thinking about." The smell of his filthy breath and revolting clothes hung in her mind, but she brushed him out of her thoughts. "He's just a drunk. I wish I'd kicked him harder. He'll be dead soon; he doesn't stand a chance. Serve him right."

Emily nodded and swallowed hard. "I want Mum," she whispered.

"I know," Maria answered, a lump in her own throat. She looked around again for the dog, but he had disappeared and the man was still shambling towards them, breathing drunken threats. Maria's heart sank. They would have to go, but what would the poor dog do? And a dog would have made a good companion. They were vulnerable out there, the two of them alone, in the dark, on an unfamiliar road. She called the dog again, in every direction, but as he didn't appear, they set off silently, alone.

It was scary. Once out of the village the girls rode side by side in the middle of the road, away from the hedgerows, where dangers might be lurking. At least they didn't have to worry about traffic, because there wasn't any. Maria wished with all her heart that they had gone back to look for the dog. How could they have left him to his fate in the empty village? And what a comfort he would have been! Maria was jumpy. Every bush waving in the wind, every rustling in the bushes made her look round in fear. Every gap in the hedge and abandoned car, of which there were a few, caused a new surge of anxiety. Once, a sudden loud barking coming from behind made her jump out of her skin, but she was not scared for long. "The dog's caught us up!" she cried delightedly.

Emily looked pleased, too. "Here, Doggie," she called. The dog wagged his feathery black tail and ran up to Emily's bike, panting. Maria coaxed him quickly towards her own bike with another biscuit. She was not having him like Emily more than her! Seeing food, he did not need to be asked twice.

"Good dog," crooned Maria, patting the dog's shaggy head. "You're such a good dog! You bit that nasty, old man, didn't you! Clever boy!" She reached down around his hairy neck and read the tag on his collar with delight. "His name's Rufus! That's so cool! I'm going to keep him. I've got my own dog!"

"He saved my life, so I think he should be my dog," argued Emily.

"No need to exaggerate," scoffed Maria, but she surprised herself once more by feeling sorry for Emily. Being grabbed by that man had been awful. "We'll share him," she conceded. "We'll both give him some of our biscuits." Emily nodded delightedly and got off her bike. Her biscuits were badly crushed, but she managed to find some larger pieces for the dog and ate the rest of the crumbs herself. Maria shared the remainder of her biscuits with Rufus, too. It could hardly be called a meal.

"He needs a drink," remarked Emily, when the biscuits had run out. It must be true. Maria didn't know much about dogs, but he was panting and he had run a long way. She hugged her precious Rufus. Who knows when he had last eaten or drunk? And she was still hungry herself. Food and water were going to have to be a priority, for them all.

The girls had to cycle a little slower now, so Rufus could keep up. It was only fair, thought Maria; he had made such a valiant effort to catch them up. She enjoyed watching Rufus pad along with them; he cheered her up with his antics. Sometimes he ran by her side or Emily's, sometimes in front, sometimes he sniffed at something in the hedgerow then ran to catch them both up again, wagging his tail and blinking at them in trust and pleasure at being in their company. It was so cool, having a dog! Maria was determined to keep him, whatever Dad said. He could hardly complain, anyway, when he heard how Rufus had protected them from that drunk. That reminded Maria of what Granny had said in her letter, that she and Grandpa would pray for angels to guard them. She grinned to herself. Maybe Rufus was an angel in disguise!

However, although the burden of fear was lifted with Rufus' presence, there were other pressing matters. They all needed a meal and somewhere safe to shelter until morning. It was completely dark now and getting colder by the minute. Maria's heart sank and her stomach rumbled as she stopped to consult her map by torchlight. The nearest village was miles away; there was no way they could make it that far tonight. But what else could they do? Maybe they could find an empty house along the road that they could break into . . . but just the thought of doing that sent a chill down Maria's spine. This was no computer game, where if you lost a life you just started again with a new one. But what choice did they have? They could knock on doors . . . but Maria quickly turned that idea away. It was too risky. She and Emily would have to manage alone, somehow, unless Mum and Dad or Grandpa found them tonight. Maria looked at her watch. It had to be possible; the cars could be coming back for them by now, surely.

As she rode on, Maria's tired mind went over and over the same problems. Food, drink, shelter . . . food, drink, shelter . . . And why wasn't there any traffic? Maybe they were the last people left on the planet. It felt like it.

Maria's heart beat faster when, round a bend in the road, they almost passed a short, wide driveway, leading to an enormous Georgian-style manor house with a white front door flanked by stone pillars. She stopped sharply and Emily drew up by her side. "A house, at last!" said

Maria, trying to sound positive, though her heart sank. She had not imagined breaking in to anything as posh as this. And there was another problem, one she didn't want to share with Emily. If they left the road, their parents couldn't find them.

"But it doesn't look like there's anyone in," objected Emily.

"That's the idea, Stupid," mocked Maria.

"We can't break in, that would be burgling . . . or breaking in."

"So what? We need somewhere to stay and there's a war, so things are different. There's no way we're going to go round knocking on doors!"

"But it's a bit big for us," wavered Emily. Maria knew what she meant. The house seemed to look disdainfully down at them with haughty black eyes. But it didn't look inhabited – at least, there were no signs of life and no cars in the drive – and they had to sleep somewhere. She stifled a yawn and made a decision. Mum and Dad would have to find them tomorrow.

"Who cares if it's big?" Maria tossed her head and held it high. "It's not that much bigger than ours! Come on, Chicken, we'll go and look round the outside – find a window to break in." She sounded bold, but didn't feel it. It was scary, just thinking about breaking into that house, but the thought of supper and feeding Rufus drove her on.

twelve

Leaving their bicycles hidden carefully between two bushes of a clipped hedge, Maria and Emily made their way quietly and uneasily round the house. In daylight, the beautiful landscaped gardens would have made a delightful place to stop and rest but now, in the darkness and because of their intentions, it took on a different perspective. Maria was tense. Every little noise made her look round fearfully. The wind whistled and moaned as if in pain and something evil seemed to be watching them on all sides, ready to pounce when they least expected it. Bushes seemed to huddle together, hiding dark secrets in their cavernous centres and trees that had not yet come into leaf rattled their skeleton branches together against the backdrop of the ominously thickening clouds.

The girls trod on well-stocked flowerbeds and rock features to look through the ground floor windows of the house. None of the curtains had been drawn, so they could dimly pick out the elegant furnishings. A grand piano sat presiding over several plush settees and armchairs in a lavish living room, a huge table and a dozen or so chairs reposed under a chandelier in the dining room and what appeared to be a ballroom with a polished wooden floor opened out on to an extensive patio.

"There doesn't seem to be anyone at home, does there?" whispered Emily, staring in at the next room – a library, filled with shelves of books from floor to ceiling.

Maria agreed. "Maybe the owners were in London on Tuesday – maybe they worked in the City and they're dead." She shivered. "Maybe that's what happened to Rufus' owners too." Emily nodded and patted Rufus in compassionate affection, then squealed and grabbed Maria in fright as a sudden noise in the shrubs nearby made her jump. "Shhh!" said Maria crossly, pushing her sister roughly away as Rufus barked and disappeared, following the rustling into the bushes. Maria and Emily stood still for a minute, melting into the shadow of the house, hearts beating loudly, but nobody came to see what the disturbance was and Rufus returned unscathed, wagging his tail. "Rabbits, probably," whispered Maria, swallowing hard. Emily nodded.

By the time they had been all round the house, Maria's fear had been replaced by frustration. The place appeared to be totally deserted, but there was simply no way in. All the windows and doors were double-glazed and locked; even on the garage. It was useless. The only good thing was an outside tap; they all had a drink, but it was cold and humiliating. "Look what we've been reduced to!" complained Maria. Emily just shrugged, but shivered as she dried her cold, wet hands on her jeans. Only Rufus didn't seem to mind; he drank thirstily out of an old bucket.

Maria had never thought to feel sorry for homeless people before. Now she did. How awful to be outside, looking in! The kitchen in that house looked so warm, so real, so totally inaccessible through the window and somewhere upstairs there would be beds; warm, soft, safe beds with crisp sheets and cosy duvets. "Couldn't we try throwing a brick through a window?" Emily suggested tiredly. Maria looked at her with surprise, trying to hide the despair she felt.

"Forget it, Miss I'm-a-Criminal-Now, they're double-glazed."

"Oh." Emily sounded worn out. Maria was furious with the house for not letting them in. She had to find a place where they could find food and rest. Suppose it was like this at every house they came to? "If we were real burglars, we'd be able to get in," sighed Emily, staring longingly through the kitchen window. "We just haven't done it before."

"Yet!" promised Maria, standing back and narrowing her eyes menacingly at the house. "Don't worry, we'll get in the next one!" She didn't like admitting that this one had defeated her. "Horrible house, anyway," was her condescending parting shot. "No character at all."

Why weren't there any more houses along this road? The girls pushed on, slower and slower. The desire to lie down and go to sleep increasingly took over Maria's thoughts. Please fetch us, please fetch us, please fetch us, she begged her parents silently over and over again in time with the turning pedals. She was glad of Rufus' gentle companionship. And suddenly, she discovered with surprise that she was glad to have Emily's company too. For one thing, it would have been unimaginably scary to do this journey alone. For another, Emily wasn't complaining, despite all that had happened. Maria grinned to herself as she imagined being here with her best mates. They would be complaining non-stop, especially Michelle. Trudi would probably be going well over the top and doing a lot of screaming and the chances of either of them following her ideas, however sensible, were remote. In fact, mused Maria, maybe Emily wasn't such a bad sister as she'd thought. Not that she had any intention of telling her!

A little further on, as they stopped at an eerily silent junction, Maria noticed something moving in the road a little way ahead. She indicated to Emily to stop. They squinted together through the darkness. "It looks like someone on a bike," whispered Emily.

Maria nodded. "They're going the same way as us." The first person they had seen since leaving Parrin Green! They couldn't see if it was male or female from this distance, but Maria was in no mood for taking chances.

"Do you think they've seen us?" asked Emily, sounding scared. Maria shook her head.

"I don't think so. But I don't want to take any chances. We've got to pass them, so we'll have to take them by surprise. You follow right behind me," she whispered. "We cycle up in silence. Then, just before I get to the person, I'll put on a sudden sprint and you follow, OK? Then they won't know we're there till we've gone."

Emily nodded, tiredly, her face pale in the darkness.

"What about Rufus?" she asked.

"He'll be OK; he sorted that old man, remember?" Maria reached down to pat Rufus, who was sitting beside her, panting. He leant his head against her knee. The girls smiled at each other. For the first time in her life, as far as she could remember, Maria felt a touch of friendship with Emily. Just a little. But the smiles had been real. Maria took a deep breath. Her heart was in her mouth. "Ready? Go!"

The quiet ride went perfectly. But as Maria speeded up, Rufus, deciding that this was a game for his benefit, started to jump around and bark loudly. Maria was alarmed. He had completely ruined the element of surprise that she was counting on. "Rufus, get out of the way!" she hissed, but Rufus was enjoying himself and had no intention of stopping.

thirteen

The person on the bike stopped and looked round at the commotion. There was no mistaking him. Maria nearly fell off her bike with surprise as she screeched to a halt, narrowly avoiding collision with Emily. "It's you!" she exclaimed.

"You've got a bike!" cried Emily, slamming on her brakes and staring in amazement at Arthur and the rickety old model he had in his possession.

"Maria and Emily!" exclaimed Arthur, equally amazed. "And you've got a dog!" He grinned even more broadly than when they had first met him. "Wow, it's great to see you – it's great to see anybody!" He sounded relieved, pleased. Maria wasn't sure what to think. Rufus barked suspiciously at him.

"It's all right, Rufus," Emily reassured him. "Friends." At this, Rufus went up to Arthur and held up his paw to be shaken. Maria tried not to laugh with the others, but couldn't help smiling. Rufus just had to be the best dog ever!

"Hey! What a great dog!" exclaimed Arthur, patting Rufus. "I didn't know you lived here! Everyone else seems to have disappeared."

"We don't live here," hesitated Maria. There was an embarrassing pause. She fiddled with the handlebars, torn between natural distrust towards strangers and thinking how good it would be to have someone to talk to. Emily spared her the decision.

"We're cycling to our cottage," she said. "We've had to leave our home. We don't live at the cottage – we just go there for holidays, but our parents are there – or nearly there – and our grandparents too, because of London getting bombed. We sort of got left behind, by mistake."

"Left behind by mistake!" repeated Arthur, attempting to make sense of Emily's explanation. "What a terrible thing to happen. I'm so sorry." There was another pause. Maria gave Emily a warning look, which meant don't tell him any more. She was getting nervous. Maybe they ought to go.

"Come on, Em," said Maria. "We need to get on." The girls got back on their bikes, as did Arthur.

"Well, it looks like we're heading in the same direction," he said, beaming. "I know this old bike's not up to much, but maybe we could cycle along together, for a while at least?" Maria hesitated. In a way, they would be less vulnerable with a male companion, but only if he was trustworthy. He seemed friendly enough, but you could never tell. And like he said, his ancient, rusty old bike was rubbish. Plus he was religious. But then, it was lonely out there and it would be difficult to refuse.

"OK," she shrugged and the others grinned. Maria surprised herself by realising how relieved she felt too. Granny's angels came to mind again and she laughed aloud. If Arthur was an angel, then God had a sense of humour!

"What are you laughing at?" questioned Emily, puzzled.

"Nothing!" But Maria continued to grin to herself as they set off once more in the darkness.

"Is it far to your cottage?" asked Arthur presently, as they rode along side by side.

"You could say that," answered Maria, shortly.

"It's at Callum, not that far from Dover," Emily chipped in. "So we can go most of the way together!" Trust her, thought Maria, glaring darkly at her sister, but Emily didn't seem to notice.

"Really?" said Arthur, beaming again, his white teeth shining in the darkness. "That's great! I was starting to feel rather lonely. The Lord is with me, of course, but it's not the same as human company!"

Maria grimaced to herself. Now, thanks to Emily's big mouth, they were saddled with this mad stranger until Dover. She shrugged mentally. Well, they could dump him if he got too much. They would still have Rufus. She deliberately rode a little in front, but before long she was furious to hear Emily and Arthur chatting like old friends. To start with, they compared schools and families. He made her laugh with tales of his home in Africa and of his little sisters. Maria would not have admitted to being jealous, but that was how she felt. Then Emily told Arthur about their parents and grandparents, their ride to town that morning, the burglars, the drunk and Rufus. To cap it all, Maria was enraged to hear Emily blaming her for their predicament. If they had stayed at home as Emily had wanted to, she informed Arthur, they wouldn't be having to be doing this journey. Maria fumed. Any new benevolent feelings that she had felt towards her sister vanished like ice-cream on a hot day. She turned round.

"You forgot to say that the burglars would probably have raped you and killed you while you were waiting at home," she interrupted viciously.

"We could have got away!" retorted Emily. "And now we'd be at the cottage!"

"How do you know? If it wasn't for me, you might be tied up or being tortured at this very minute – or your dead body might be floating in a river somewhere!"

Emily didn't reply. She's embarrassed now, Maria smirked to herself. Serve her right, little sneak! And that Arthur probably is too! However, after chatting quietly to Emily for a while, Arthur cycled up to join Maria. "Do you have any plans for tonight?" he asked politely.

Maria didn't know whether to be annoyed or pleased. "Do you?" she asked shortly.

There was a pause. Arthur sounded a little taken aback. "Well, I was pacing myself to cycle as far as I could," Arthur told her, "but as we've agreed to join forces, I'm happy to fit in with you."

"I'm looking for a house to break into as soon as possible," Maria informed him airily. "We need food and drink as well as shelter. We've tried one house already, but we couldn't get in."

"Oh," said Arthur. He didn't sound particularly happy about her plans, but made no comment. Maria was pleased. Wimp! She would show him who was boss! She told him briefly about the house that they couldn't get in to. Then, feeling a bit mean that she had been rude, she admitted that the last couple of days had really stressed her out and she was tired. To this, Arthur nodded sympathetically.

"Anyway, we'll have to stop soon so Rufus can rest," added Maria. "We can't make him run all night." At the thought of rest, a wave of tiredness swept over her and she yawned widely.

It wasn't long before a dark rectangle loomed up above the hedgerows ahead. "There's another house up there!" called out Emily wearily and she put on a small spurt of energy. Maria did not know whether to laugh or cry – a house, at last – maybe more than one to choose from! This time, she promised herself, gritting her teeth, they would get in somehow, no matter what. She would show her parents that she didn't need them!

But her disappointment was intense. There had been a fire. Two cottages, semi-detached, stood grey and forlorn in the dark night. The fire had evidently begun in the first house; its windows had blown out and soot stained the bricks above the windows. A hole in the roof gaped open to the elements and a rose bush by the remains of the front door had died, black and twisted. The other house looked pretty bleak, too. The fire appeared to have spread across the roof; piles of slate tiles lay higgledy-piggledy, on the small front gardens, where they had slid off. Maria sat on her bike, silently taking in the sad sight. It would have been better not to have found a house than to have their hopes dashed a second time, she decided wearily. Exhaustion, physical and emotional, washed over her and she leant over the handlebars of her bike, buffeted by the strengthening wind, trying to hide the despair she felt. Her legs ached, her arms ached, she was getting cold and she was so, so tired. When would this nightmare end?

"God will provide," said Arthur gently, but this was the last thing Maria wanted to hear right now.

"Why didn't God provide one of these houses then?" she snapped.

"Well," began Arthur, "it's not really right to break into people's houses, you know. I bet you were upset when your house was broken into."

"I loved it!" snapped Maria again. She was in no mood to put up with this goody-goody stuff.

"I bet you didn't though, did you? God will provide another way, he always does. Maybe there will be a barn or something where we can sleep."

"A barn?" cried Maria. "Are you out of your mind? Do you seriously think I'm going to sleep in a barn when there are empty houses around with beds and kitchens stocked full of food? What do you take me for, some kind of religious wimp?"

As soon as she said that, she regretted it, but she did not intend to apologise. He deserved it really, she convinced herself, with all his high and mighty God stuff. Arthur didn't reply. Emily just sat on her bike, staring at her feet and Rufus lay down on the road. Maria felt responsible for them both. She needed to get them to a place of warmth and safety. Whatever she had said earlier, it was at least partly her fault that they were in this mess. "Come on, Emily," she said brusquely, lifting her head high and cycling off again, not daring to look and see if the others were following. Tears stung her eyes and throat. For how much longer was this nightmare going to last?

fourteen

Maria did not get far. As she passed the second house, she paused. The first one may have been badly burnt, but apart from the roof, its neighbour looked relatively unscathed; maybe it just looked black inside because it was dark. She shivered. The wind was cold. Whatever that stupid Arthur intended to do, she was going to sleep in a house! Maria dumped her bike on the grass verge and, without so much as glancing at the others, she walked up the short path to the second cottage, dodging the fallen tiles.

The brown patterned curtains in the front window did not even look smoky and the freshly-painted yellow front door looked as good as new. Encouraged, she went round a gate to the back. It was pitch black. "Rufus!" she called and he ran up to her, trusting her in the dark night. She could hear the others talking, probably about her, but she didn't care. The noise made by the gate slamming shut behind her made Maria jump nervously, but she was determined to see this through. Having Rufus with her gave her courage. She rummaged in her bag for her torch and looked warily round by its narrow beam. There was a path running through a small garden, beyond which were fields. The back door of the house was made of solid wood, but Maria shone her torch through what appeared to be the kitchen window. She could make out the sink and beyond it a wooden table and chairs. Nothing looked damaged by fire. Her heart beat faster. She had to get in! She went to the back door and tried the handle, unsuccessfully. That was hardly surprising, but on an impulse, Maria lifted the doormat and there was a key! "Yes!" she said aloud, eyes glinting. She held it up jubilantly then realised that it wasn't the right sort of key for the lock. But she wasn't ready to give up yet.

"Here, boy!" she called to Rufus, who had been sniffing round the little garden and, head held high and totally ignoring the others, she marched through the gate and tried the key in the front door. With a sharp click, the door opened.

Maria was triumphant. She had sure shown the others! "Coming in?" she called loftily and without waiting for a reply she stepped inside, Rufus eagerly pushing past her, wagging his tail.

Inside, there was no sign of the fire that had destroyed next door, apart from the stale smell of smoke, but Maria paused in the dark hall, heart racing, in case anyone was at home. "Anybody here?" she called out. To her immense relief nobody came, even when she flashed her torch up the stairs and through the open living room door. She started to relax. Rufus leaned his head against her knee and licked her hand, which made her laugh. "This is our home for tonight, Rufus!" she told him jubilantly, scratching his dear head. The carpet felt beautifully soft under her aching feet. Her conscience stung a little as she glanced at a group of photographs on a wall – after all, real people lived here, but surely they wouldn't mind lending them their house for the night, considering the circumstances?

Maria opened the door at the end of the hall. It was the kitchen/dining room that she had seen from outside. She turned her attention to the cupboards. Tins and packets of food! Loads of them! Maria was so excited that she did a little dance. She could feed Rufus! They could all have a meal! Then she could go to sleep . . .

A creak at the kitchen door made Maria jump, but it was only Emily, cautiously peering in. Maria grinned at her sister. "Coming in?"

"But it's burnt down," objected Emily.

"Use your eyes, Stupid!" replied Maria scornfully. "It smells a bit of smoke, but that's from next door. It just looks black 'cause it's dark. It's smaller than we're used to, but . . ."

"Who cares!" finished Emily, making a beeline for the cupboards while Maria filled a chipped enamel pie dish with water for Rufus. "There's everything!" Emily squealed happily, rifling through the stacks of hidden treasure. "Orange juice, loads of tins of stuff – rice pudding, peaches, baked beans, tomatoes . . . what's this? Oh, disgusting, corned beef." She looked up. "Sorry what I said about you to Arthur," she said.

Maria looked round in surprise. "Pardon?"

"I said, sorry about what I said to Arthur," repeated Emily quietly, looking down. "About you. You were right really."

Maria was dumbstruck. Now that had to be a first – an apology from Emily! She shrugged. "That's OK," she replied magnanimously and turned her attention to the bread bin. A whole sliced loaf and – oh joy! – a pack of six currant buns! She checked the best before date. Another two days to go – they wouldn't last as long as that! Food! "Have a bun!" she said, tearing them apart. She handed two stuck together to Emily with a grin and took a big bite out of another two herself. Maria could hardly believe it, Emily had apologised. They laughed.

Maria was exultant. Who needed to be fetched by stupid parents? This trip was not turning out to be so bad after all. Wait till her mates heard about this – her first ever break-in had been a success! Rufus whined and lifted his paw when he saw Maria eating. "It's OK, Rufus," Maria reassured him. "You can have something too!" She gave him the corned beef, which disappeared in two mouthfuls, followed by a tin of ham, which he also ate greedily.

"Shall I go and tell Arthur?" asked Emily, her mouth full of second bun. "I said I'd let him know."

"Let him know what?"

"If it's OK."

"If you want," shrugged Maria. "Why should I care?" Then she realised that she did care. She couldn't say why, but she didn't want to lose his company. He would probably leave them if she and Emily stayed here. She grabbed the last two buns and took them out to him, but he just stood there, looking solemn.

"I can't eat those," he said, shaking his head. "They

belong to somebody else." Maria was exasperated.

"Suppose this is what God's giving you?" she said, trying to keep calm.

"It's stealing, Maria," he explained gently. "I'm a Christian and that would be breaking God's commandments." Emily ran back indoors. Maria was losing patience. "So what if it is? Who's going to mind? The buns will be mouldy in a couple of days – they'll only get wasted."

"Maria, it's not just about the buns. I have to answer to God for decisions I make and I don't feel happy about going into someone's home uninvited and eating their food."

"What are you going to do then, starve?" How infuriating could a person get? Arthur did not reply. Maria felt like going back into the house and shutting the door in his obstinate face, but she hung on, trying to think of a way she could persuade him to stay.

Arthur was obviously deep in thought, too. His brow was furrowed and serious. He did not look as if he belonged there, in his school suit, holding the rusty old bike. It occurred to Maria that he must be really cold; he wasn't even wearing a jumper. And he was turning down this little house! The two of them stood there in silence, Maria impatient, Arthur solemn, but no less determined. Rufus came out, wagging his tail and sat contentedly down on Maria's feet, licking round his face. The meal had obviously gone down well. She bent down and hugged the dog, then smiled at Arthur too. She could not stay cross for long with Rufus about! Arthur smiled back.

It was a deep, peaceful smile that somehow reached right inside him. Maria was puzzled. It was like it didn't matter to him whether he slept in a bed or in a barn or even if he ate or not. She and Emily were the ones who had food and a house to sleep in, but somehow, he was the one who seemed to have it all. Maria did not know what to think.

It was Emily who broke the silence. She came rushing out of the house with something in her hand. It was a decorated plaque. "Read this," she urged Arthur, shoving the plaque into his hands.

fifteen

Arthur looked at the plaque and read its bold statement aloud. "Jesus is Lord of our Home". Emily nodded enthusiastically. "See!" she said. "You can come in too!" There was another pause, heavy in the darkness. Then Arthur gave a huge beam, which was like the sun breaking through after a dull day. "I guess you two are right!" he chuckled. "Maybe this is God's provision!" Maria did not understand why the Jesus thing had made him change his mind, nor did she care. She nearly skipped with relief. Together the three of them wheeled their bikes round to the back of the house and made themselves at home.

It was great to be out of the cold and the wind and to stretch their aching limbs. Admittedly, it was just as dark indoors and pretty chilly too, but it was still and peaceful and it felt safe. Emily showed Arthur excitedly round the house, laughing at Rufus, who pushed them out of the way, wanting to be first in every room. Maria followed quietly; she was just glad that Emily seemed to have forgotten why they were there. There were two bedrooms upstairs; one painted yellow with a double bed and a smaller pink room with twin beds. "Me and Maria can sleep in this room," Emily announced happily. For once in her life, Maria didn't argue. Normally, she would have done, just so that Emily didn't get her way, but tonight she decided she couldn't be bothered. "You can have the double bed in the big room, Arthur," Emily informed him and he graciously nodded and smiled. How pathetic, being told what to do by a little kid, thought Maria scathingly, but she kept her thoughts to herself.

It looked as if old people lived in the cottage. Everything was old-fashioned, from the frilly bedspreads to the ancient white cooker, but it was clean enough, as well as the travellers could see by torchlight. The occupants must have left in a hurry at night, Emily deduced, because everything was neat except that the double bed had not been made. Maria sneered. She did not care why the old fogies had left; all that mattered was that they were not there now.

The most exciting discovery, apart from the abundant supply of food, was an open fire in the living room, with logs piled neatly in a basket and a gleaming copper box full of coal. Maria immediately felt her spirits rise. "We can have a fire!" she said with glee, rubbing her cold hands in anticipation.

"Cook food on it!" yelled Emily in excitement.

"Hot drinks!" added Arthur.

"Woof!" barked Rufus and they all fell about laughing.

It wasn't long before Arthur had a roaring fire going. As he added more coal and wood, the crackling flames spread and grew, lighting up the floral wallpaper, the ancient chintz sofa and the assorted old-fashioned jumble of furniture, pictures and ornaments that covered every available surface of the living room. Emily chattered animatedly and Maria found it strangely exciting, too. It was almost as if they had passed into another world, outside of reality. Arthur grinned at her and she grinned back. Who needed adults when they were having fun like this? She tossed her head in independence as she and Emily went to the kitchen in search of something for supper.

Maria was all for just heating up something quick from a tin, but Emily, who had been to camp with the Scouts the previous summer, wanted to do things properly. Having found some eggs and sausages in the fridge that still looked edible, she attempted to fry them over the fire, but the flames were too hot and the food burnt quickly, filling the room with choking smoke. Even Emily laughed at the inedible, blackened mess that was left in the pan. Admitting defeat, she tipped two tins of rice pudding in a saucepan and placed it on the edge of the fire to heat up.

While they were waiting, Arthur picked up the frying pan with the burnt remains and pretended to be presenting a cookery programme. He found a paper bag for a chef's hat and, with a flourish, presented the sausages and eggs in the pan for all to see. "Here we have an exciting dish called . . . what are you going to call it, chef?"

"Sausages and eggs," giggled Emily.

"Oeufs and pork, burnt à la cottage," invented Maria. They hooted with laughter as Arthur tried to scrape the eggs off the bottom of the saucepan with a fish slice.

"Would Madam like to try a delicious forkful?" he

offered Emily, attempting a cut glass accent, which could hardly have sounded more ridiculous. "No? Then how about a little rice pudding, from a secret recipe?" He picked up the pan from where it should have been simmering over the hot coals, but unfortunately, it too, had burned on the bottom. Now, as Arthur stirred it, black bits mixed in with the creamy pudding and the smell of burnt milk filled the air.

"It's burnt!" yelled Emily, laughing.

"Pass me a bucket!" grimaced Maria, holding her nose and running for the door to fan air into the room.

"I can safely say," said Arthur, pompously, "that that's the worst rice pudding I have ever seen in my life! My compliments to the chef!" Maria and Emily whooped with laughter and Arthur joined in. It wasn't really that funny, but the relief of feeling safe and warm made them all slightly euphoric. Even Rufus barked and wagged his tail, but he turned his nose up at the burnt offerings, which made them laugh all the more.

"I'll do boiled eggs!" decided Emily, but Arthur and Maria forced Emily to give up on the cooking. Dumping the burnt pans in the sink, Maria fetched the loaf of bread from the kitchen and they contented themselves instead with toasting slice after slice on forks over the glowing fire. Some of that got burnt too, and so did their fingers, but it went down well, buttered, followed by tinned peaches with thick, sweet condensed milk and ginger biscuits from a snowman cookie jar.

After the meal, a feeling of well-being filled Maria. She stretched lazily out on the patterned rug in front of the fire. Rufus, who had had his fair share of toast, laid his head adoringly on her knee and sighed contentedly. She fondled his head and silky ears, grinning to herself. The "angels" were turning out to be pretty cool! Rufus was just the best dog ever and Arthur was a laugh.

But something was puzzling her about Arthur. She leant up on her elbow. "Why are you going to France, Arthur? Didn't I hear you say your home's in Africa?"

Arthur looked lazily round from his slouch on the armchair. "My parents are in Paris at the moment, with my Dad's job. I guess they couldn't fetch me from school, so I'm going to find them."

"What if they're on the way?"

"They'd want me to use my common sense – it's much easier for me to get to them than for them to get to me. I've got three little sisters at school in Paris, you see. I did wait a while, but by yesterday there weren't many of us left at school and things were getting difficult. When we had a talk from the Head about having to go easy on the food, I decided it was time to leave." Arthur grinned. "If I had to starve somewhere, I didn't intend to do it at school!"

"That was brave of you," said Emily, from her curled-up position on the settee. "I wouldn't have dared leave on my own."

"Well, it's only Paris," countered Arthur. "I haven't got to get to Japan, like one of my friends!"

"So what were you doing when the planes came?" asked Maria.

"We were in the middle of a cross-country run – we got

back in record time! It was awful, though," he added, more sombrely. "One of my best mate's brothers was at Westminster. He probably didn't make it . . ." Arthur traced the green, pink and brown pattern on the armchair with his finger. "What about you?"

"We were at home. Our dad thought it was an air show!" Hearing Emily sniff, Maria decided to leave off the subject of families. "Have you any idea where the planes came from?" she asked Arthur.

"Personally, I haven't a clue, but someone said they thought they came from France."

"France?" Maria made a face. "But the French are on our side! Unless your parents sent them to get rid of you!"

"Terrorists could have hijacked them."

"Don't be pathetic! You saw how many planes there were! The French aren't that dim."

"Well, don't look at me, it wasn't my idea, I heard it on the news. Someone thought the planes could have been on a warship in the English Channel and the ship was hijacked."

This was out of the girls' realm. They made "How should we know?" faces at each other. Arthur shrugged. "I know it sounds incredible . . ."

"You're not kidding!" said Maria. But it could have happened. It seemed like terrorists could do just about anything these days. She stared at the crackling fire. Its warmth could not quell the chill that shivered down her spine. "Maybe there's a proper war about to start and we don't know about it," she said uneasily. "Dad said something about there could be a war, before he left."

"That would explain why everywhere's deserted round here," agreed Arthur.

Maria nodded slowly. "Maybe everyone's been evacuated or something."

"We could see if we could find a radio," suggested Emily. "Get some news."

"Good thinking," nodded Arthur. "We'll have a search."

"In the morning," countered Maria, "when it's light." The others nodded. Maria was not even sure if she wanted to know. The thought of being caught up in a war made her stomach heave. She had seen pictures on the news of places where there were wars. It wasn't nice.

The three of them lapsed into silence. Maria watched the hypnotic, ever-changing patterns of the flames. At first the fire had seemed a benevolent force to provide them with light and warmth, hot tea and toast and even entertain them with its beautiful shades of orange and blue. But as Arthur added another shovel of coal, the leaping flames seemed to reveal another side. Instead of kindly warmth Maria sensed an angry, destructive force burning with hatred, waiting to be set free to kill, to maim, to bring suffering and destruction.

sixteen

Only the hiss and spit of the fire and the whine of the wind in the chimney disturbed the uneasy stillness in the dark living room. "Do you think there will be a war?" asked Emily eventually. Maria shrugged and looked away. She did not want to talk about it. Arthur hesitated too.

"Well," he said at last, "Jesus says in the Bible that in the end times, wars and rumours of wars will increase. But whether this is going to be a war, or just a rumour of a war, I'm afraid I don't know. There are certainly plenty of wars in other countries."

"The end times?" asked Emily, sounding puzzled. "What's that?"

"It's the time at the end of the world as we know it, before Jesus comes back." Emily stared at Arthur in total absence of comprehension. Maria squirmed. She had almost forgotten that Arthur was religious. Why did he have to bring up all this stupid stuff now? Maybe he came from one of those weird sects who brainwash all their followers then make suicide pacts. She decided it was time to change the subject.

"Where did you get your bike, Arthur?"

"Now that was a real find!" he grinned. "It was at Parrin

Green. I thought I'd go to the church, but there wasn't anybody about." Maria nodded. She had found that out for herself. "And there was this old bike, leaning up against the wall, so . . ."

"You nicked it!" Maria butted in triumphantly. "You stole the vicar's bike!"

Arthur frowned. "I hadn't thought of it like that," he admitted. "It was like it had been left there for me." Maria burst out laughing, but Arthur looked thoughtful. "It doesn't sound very good, does it? But I'm sure the vicar wouldn't mind. If it was his. After all, what belongs to him belongs to God." He grinned. Maria stopped laughing and screwed her face up at him.

"After all you said to me outside about God's commandments! You hypocrite! What's the vicar supposed to do when he gets back and finds his bike's gone missing?" Emily laughed; even Arthur seemed to think it was amusing, but Maria didn't intend to let him get away with it as easily as that. "Are you trying to tell me it's OK for you to nick stuff from other Christians?"

"Well, you may be right about the bike, Maria," admitted Arthur. "When I get to Paris I'll ask Dad to send a cheque to replace it, although I really do believe it was left there for me. The Lord knew I'd need it." Maria scowled, but Arthur leaned forward keenly and his eyes sparkled in the dancing firelight. "How many real Christians do you know?"

"Our grandparents," Emily answered immediately. "They're praying for us. And they left their back door open when they went away so that anyone could go in their house if they needed shelter. At least, we think that's why."

"Really?" grinned Arthur, looking pleased. "That's great!"

Maria tried to think of something to say, but she couldn't. Granny and Grandpa were real Christians, she couldn't deny it. So she kept quiet, but inwardly she was filled with disdain. Who did this smug boy think he was, making out that he was dead holy, then stealing when it suited him? But to her annoyance, the conversation continued without her; Emily seemed to have been properly taken in by his charm.

"That's why you didn't mind coming in here after all, wasn't it?" Emily asked him eagerly. "Because the people here are Christians too and you knew they wouldn't mind sharing their home and food with you!"

"That's it exactly!" Arthur agreed warmly. "I would really like to have asked them first, but one day I'll meet them in heaven, then I can say thanks!" He laughed, as if in anticipation of a happy reunion. Maria cringed. Personally, she hoped she would never meet them — it would be just too embarrassing. She got up.

"I'm going to bed," she said. Not only had the fire lost its charm, the conversation had lost its appeal too.

It was a strange feeling, lying fully clothed on someone else's bed, in a strange house, in a sleeping bag, covered with a pink frilly bedspread. Maria nearly ditched the bedspread in disgust, but in the end, warmth won over style, and after all, she grimaced to herself, nobody could see her.

"I feel a bit like Goldilocks," yawned Emily, teeth chattering in the sudden chill of the borrowed bedroom. "I hope the bears don't come home and find us sleeping in their beds!"

Well, thought Maria, if they do, they can blame Arthur, who said that it was OK for Christians to share their stuff. They would find him first, anyway, because he was in their bed. Rufus licked Maria's hand lovingly. She stretched her aching body out as best as she could with the dog's heavy body taking up so much room and fondled his hairy head in smug satisfaction – he had chosen her bed, not Emily's! What a luxury to be in bed, with her own dog! For a few seconds, Maria thought of their parents. Maybe they were out there somewhere looking for them, missing out on their precious beauty sleep. Well, serve them right, she decided. They should have come earlier; she'd show them that she could cope perfectly well without them! She wriggled over, wedging her back against Rufus' warm body. She yawned widely, listening to the wind, which couldn't touch her here. Surely she had never, ever been as tired as this before! The pillow was gently scented and gloriously soft. Rufus sighed contentedly and Maria went to sleep with a smile on her face.

A tremendous crash awoke her at first light. She sat bolt upright in bed in a cold sweat, her heart thumping, wondering what could have woken her. Rufus had jumped up and was growling deeply in his throat. But all that could now be heard was rain beating on the windowpanes and wind howling round the house and in the chimney. Gradually Maria's heart returned to its normal rhythm.

Whatever had woken her had gone. Maybe it had been a clap of thunder; it was certainly stormy outside. Not a good day for a cycle ride, she sighed to herself, as the reality of the day seeped into her sleep-sodden mind. The wind was unsettling. It seemed to have a hidden agenda. It was shrieking furiously outside and scouring the chimney like a demented banshee, searching for something or someone; maybe her and Emily. The wind also threw violent gusts of rain against the windows and whipped round the little house angrily. It had not got them yet, but it seemed to be waiting for them. Maria didn't like it. Neither did Rufus. Incredibly, Emily was still asleep. Maria crept further down into her sleeping bag, unwilling to face the day just yet, vaguely wondering who could possibly have chosen such awful rosebud wallpaper.

The lie-in did not last long. With another huge gust of wind, a terrifying tearing noise ripped through the house, loud and near, followed almost immediately by an awful crash, which Maria recognised with a rush of fear as the same sound that had woken her, though louder this time. Something enormous had fallen. Rufus leaped off the bed, barking and bounded down the stairs. Maria struggled out of her sleeping bag in a panic and grabbed her trainers. Emily woke, screaming in terror and Arthur ran out on to the landing, shouting, "Get out! The house is breaking up!"

Emily, still screaming, ran for the stairs as another dreadful sound of ripping came from immediately behind her. Maria turned and stood transfixed in horror. The back wall of the bedroom was tearing away from the house before her eyes. It wavered where it stood for a second, then collapsed in what seemed like slow motion, leaving a massive hole through which Maria could see the back garden and the green fields beyond in the grey, early morning light. The wind was exultant in its victory. It tore at the loose wallpaper, dislodged another handful of bricks and slid the ornaments on the chest of drawers across the polished wood. Arthur reached in, grabbed Maria's wrist and pulled her towards the stairs just as a beam and a pile of bricks crashed through the ceiling behind them, crushing the beds in which she and Emily had been lying just seconds ago. A cascade of plaster and dust clattered to the floor. Arthur and Maria coughed and choked as they made for the stairs. "Where's Rufus?" yelled Maria above the noise of the wind and rain as they burst out of the house, but nobody knew.

Maria stood with Arthur and Emily, scared and shivering in the road, out of reach of falling masonry. The cold wind, the driving rain and the shock of their narrow escape took her breath away. Seeing the houses in daylight was a shocking revelation. There was virtually no roof left and the chimney was leaning at a frightening angle. What if it had fallen in on them last night, as they slept? The thought chilled her to the bone.

And where was Rufus? Maria looked desperately around. Emily hadn't seen him either. Maybe he had got out of the back of the house, through a hole in the wall . . . Maria's heart beat faster when he didn't appear. She ran a little way up the road and back looking for him, calling his name, but he didn't come. Surely he couldn't still be inside? Tears sprang to her eyes. With a loud creaking and groaning another beam and a pile of bricks smashed from the roof through the little house. "No, no!" Maria screamed in horror. The wind snatched away her cry with a loud sneer.

Then, as if unsatisfied with the damage it had already caused, the gale gave another deafening, violent burst, which nearly knocked Emily off her feet. The three watched in horror as the blackened upstairs wall of the first cottage, creaking and groaning in useless protest, was torn away from the house as effortlessly as if it were made of gingerbread. Seconds later, with a loud crash and another cloud of dust, the precarious pile of bricks collapsed in a tragic heap. The floor of the exposed bedroom creaked and bowed and the contents rattled, ashamed and embarrassed at showing their nakedness to the world outside.

Its energy spent, the wind seemed to ease a little as the dust settled. A sacrifice had been made and its anger was appeased. Layers of brick and cladding lay in sad defeat in the little gardens. Tiles lay scattered on the wet grass. The roof was all but a memory. The harmless houses stood forlorn, defeated against the might of the giant, baring their inner secrets for all to see, humbled and broken.

"That's what you call a narrow escape," yelled Arthur above the noise of the wind and rain, wiping his brow. For the first time since they had met him, Arthur looked visibly shaken, but Maria hardly noticed. Tears poured unashamedly down her cheeks. Rufus was still missing.

seventeen

Masonry crumbled and dust blew in the stiff, gusting wind, sticking in their throats and making them cough. "I need my shoes!" wailed Emily. "And my coat and my sleeping bag and all my things!" All three of them were getting colder and wetter, standing in the driving rain with no jackets. Arthur, like Maria, had managed to save his shoes and he seemed to have found himself an old jumper, but it was precious little protection against the elements. Maria hardly noticed. All she could think of was Rufus. Her precious dog! His gentle eyes looking trustingly up at her were all she could see in her mind. She choked back a sob.

"I'm going back in to find Rufus!" she yelled to the others.

"No!" screamed Emily, shaking with fear and the cold. Arthur grabbed Maria's arm.

"Wait a minute," he said. "Wait till it settles." She shook him off and stood in desperate indecision. But the wind had done its worst and seemed to be quietening down. Maria ran up to the open front door. She tried to call Rufus' name, but the sound stuck in her throat.

Arthur came up behind her and gently moved her out

of the way. "I'll go in. Your sister needs you. And anyway, if I die, I'll go to heaven. I'm not sure about you!" He gave a little smile. Maria was not sure if he was serious or not, but she let him go.

She watched him enter the lounge. He came out and shook his head at her, then, crunching through rubble, disappeared into the kitchen. Maria flinched and stood back as another tile slid off the roof and crashed near her, then to her horror, from the direction of the kitchen came the noise of a loud slide, a bang, a clatter of things falling and a yell from Arthur. Emily ran up. "No, no," she sobbed. Maria went white with fright.

"Arthur!" she yelled. "Are you OK?" There was no response. Just deathly silence, then the sound of another slide and more things falling.

"I'm going in," said Maria determinedly.

"No!" sobbed Emily, running up to her. "Not you too, Maria, no! Don't leave me here!" She clutched her jumper, but Maria roughly shook her off. "Go and stand in the road!" she ordered her.

Maria stood in the draughty hall, peering through the cloud of dust. Incredibly, the photographs were still hanging on the wall, albeit at odd angles. "Arthur?" called Maria quietly, then more desperately, "Arthur? Rufus?" She put her arms over her head as a fountain of plaster clattered on to the floor behind her.

"Here, in the kitchen," came a low voice. "Don't shout! You'll bring the house down!"

"Sorry," whispered Maria, relieved. At least Arthur was alive. But her relief was mixed with horror when she saw that the back of the house was more than less in the garden, leaving the cottage looking like a dolls' house with a removable back. Maybe that was the first crash that had woken her up. A burst of rain swept in and she shivered. How safe she had felt there! She looked nervously round. Arthur was crouched on the floor by the table. "Is he there?" she asked anxiously, meaning Rufus. "What was that noise? Are you OK?"

"He's here, hiding under the table," said Arthur quietly, stifling a sneeze. "Some plaster fell. We're both fine. But he won't come out."

"Why not? Is he injured?" Maria went hot and cold.

"I don't think so. I think he's just frightened. I tried to crawl under and get him out, but he just moved further back against the wall. I can't make him budge." Maria got right down on to the floor. It was such a relief to see her dear dog alive! Tears sprung to her eyes. Seeing her there seemed to comfort him. He whined, but wagged his shaggy tail, showering dust in all directions. She talked reassuringly to him and he took a cautious step towards her. Maria smiled and begged him to keep walking, but when a shower of dust and bits of plaster cascaded down from the ceiling behind her, he quickly huddled back into his corner, whimpering. Maria turned and looked up to the source of the fall and her eyes opened wide. The wardrobe from the little bedroom was perched over a hole in the ceiling above them, held up only by a bowed wooden beam, which was creaking under its unaccustomed load. If something gave way, the wardrobe would fall into the kitchen. Anything, or anyone underneath it would be crushed. She pointed it out to Arthur. He nodded.

"It slid there when I came in," he said quietly. "Bits keep falling down. We need to get out of here as soon as we can."

Maria anxiously turned her attention to the table under which Rufus was sitting. She thought quickly. If they couldn't pull Rufus out, maybe they could move the table. But the table was lying under a fallen piece of wall.

"We could move the table," whispered Maria, "and prop the wall up with something else."

"With what?" Arthur queried. Maria looked desperately round. Good point. She thought of another plan.

"We'll coax him out with some food." She got up slowly, stifling a cough. The dust was getting in her eyes, up her nose and tickling her throat. Keeping an eye on the hole in the ceiling, she gingerly opened the food cupboard and found a tin of beef stew, all the while talking reassuringly to Rufus. Vaguely in the background she could hear Emily calling them, though it seemed far away. Plaster continued to fall through the ceiling alarmingly, sometimes in small trickles, sometimes in heart-stopping bursts. Once, the cascade was accompanied by a loud creaking and Maria covered her head with her arms, while she heard things upstairs falling and furniture sliding overhead. Her heart was thumping and her hands were shaking as she shook the dust out of the old bowl that she had used for Rufus last night, opened the tin and mashed the meat up clumsily with a fork.

"Come on, Rufus," coaxed Maria, kneeling down on the

floor, holding the bowl at the edge of the table. The smell of the meat made her stomach heave. "Come on! Nice meat for breakfast!" She and Arthur exchanged an anxious glance as Rufus sniffed the bowl. "Come on, Rufus, come out, please!" she pleaded. He whined but didn't move. Maria looked at Arthur in hopeless desperation, but he had his eyes closed and his lips were moving. He's praying, thought Maria. She felt like praying herself; if ever she needed there to be a god, it was now, but she didn't know what to say. "Oh, please come out, Rufus, please . . ." she begged instead. There was silence in the little room. For a long minute the plaster stopped falling and Rufus started to creep slowly towards the bowl, sniffing.

"He's coming out!" whispered Maria excitedly, shaking Arthur, who opened his eyes.

"Hallelujah! Thank you, Lord!"

Maria carried the bowl a little further away from Rufus, towards the hall. He followed, still sniffing. As another load of plaster fell through the kitchen ceiling, Maria tensed in fear, hoping that Rufus wouldn't turn and run back under the table, but instead he made a rush for the front door and the three of them burst out together, coughing and sneezing.

"There you are, at last!" cried Emily, running up. She was a sorry sight. The wind was whipping her hair in rats' tails round her shoulders and her wet clothes were sticking to her body. Tears joined the raindrops running in rivulets down her cheeks and she was shivering violently. "You've been ages! Why didn't you answer me when I called?"

"Sorry, Emily, but the vibrations might have set off another fall," explained Arthur, as they ran quickly away from the house.

"Oh." Emily wiped her face with a wet hand. "Is Rufus OK?" In reply, Rufus barked at Maria, who put his breakfast down in the empty road. He ate the meat hungrily, keeping one eye on the house. Maria patted him and surreptitiously wiped away her own tears. The others pretended not to notice.

"He's fine," replied Arthur. "He was just frightened, that's all." He turned to Maria and patted her on the back, grinning once again. "You were brilliant – giving him food was a great idea! It was really dangerous in there. No wonder the people who lived here didn't go back in for their things!"

Maria nodded, staring at the ruins. Why hadn't they thought of that? "I didn't realise . . ." her voice trailed off. How could she have known? How could any of them have known? They weren't builders. Well, it was too late to worry about it now. She bent down to pat Rufus, who whined and hid behind her as more tiles slid off the roof. Maria turned her thoughts to the next problem. Their bags and all their things were in the house.

"What are we going to do now?" asked Emily. She was barefoot, soaked and shivering from head to toe. "My shoes and my jacket are in there. So's all my stuff – in my bag. And my brace."

"Who cares about your brace?" scoffed Maria, but she continued to stare at the forlorn remains of the house. Emily had to have her shoes. They all needed breakfast, dry clothes and jackets and she needed her hairbrush and toothbrush at the very least. She had intended to stock up with food and drink from the kitchen, too, but she had seen what it was like inside. "We can't go back in," she said slowly. "It's too dangerous."

"I didn't have anything much, anyway," said Arthur cheerfully. Maria rounded on him.

"I see you've nicked a jumper, though!" she snapped.

"Borrowed!" smiled Arthur. "When I get to Paris . . ."

"Oh, shut up!" Maria shouted savagely. "If you hadn't noticed, it's raining and Emily hasn't even got any shoes to wear!"

Arthur looked suitably repentant. "Sorry, sorry," he replied graciously. "Look, you can borrow mine if you like." He took off his shoes and offered them to Emily. Any other time it would have been funny. They were huge, black, men's shoes; they obviously weren't going to fit. Maria stared at Arthur in disbelief. Emily stared at the shoes.

"They're no good," she wailed. "I need my own!"

"They are a bit big," he admitted, looking at her feet. "I didn't realise you had such small feet." Maria struggled with herself.

"Where are they?" she asked Emily, ignoring Arthur. Stupid boy!

"By the fire I think," sniffed Emily. "In the lounge. The rest of my stuff's upstairs."

Arthur put his shoes back on. "We can't go upstairs," he told her. "Part of the roof has collapsed on your bed and there's a wardrobe about to fall through the ceiling."

Emily's eyes widened in fear. "So what are we going to do?" she wailed.

"We'd better start by praying," suggested Arthur.

"You can," said Maria. "I'm going to get Emily's shoes. Stay there, Rufus!" she commanded and before the others could say a word, she had gone.

eighteen

As Maria cycled along, setting the pace slow enough for Rufus to keep up, she wondered if she had ever felt worse in her life. She was wet through, aching all over from the unaccustomed exercise and it was hard work cycling in the gusting wind, although the effort was warming her up. The memory of all the things that she had so carefully packed and been forced to abandon filled her with anger and frustration. The empty panniers flapped at the sides of her bike in constant reminder of her destitution. What else could go wrong? She'd have to trust the route to her memory – the map was still in her lost jacket pocket. At least she had managed to save Emily's shoes, and the falling cottage walls had missed their bikes. Arthur had said it was a miracle. It was certainly a bit of luck – the only bit so far, thought Maria grimly.

There was still one glimmer of hope; maybe her parents or grandparents would find them soon, now they were back on the main road. Having an adventure was one thing, but enough was enough. Every so often a car or van passed the cyclists, which was encouraging in a way; at least they weren't the only people left alive, but every time Maria heard an engine approaching, she secretly hoped that it was one of their cars, until she thought she would burst. Every time it wasn't, the disappointment was intense. And more and more, Maria had to stop herself thinking about the planes, the mess in London, her father's surgery, her mother's handbag and the pool of blood.

For a long time nobody talked. What was there to say? thought Maria miserably. At least the wind and the rain were dying down. Maria's wet trousers stuck to her legs and she shivered involuntarily as she scanned the cloudy sky every now and then for the return of the black planes – maybe more, bigger ones this time; screaming, evil metal, with chemical weapons or even nuclear bombs . . . To escape the fear and misery, Maria forced her thoughts towards an imaginary paradise in the sun, where she played volleyball on a warm beach, laughing with Trudi and Michelle as they flirted with bronzed, fit surfers.

After a while, Arthur roused Maria from her reverie by starting to sing hymns and other religious-sounding songs she didn't recognise. She ignored him at first, although it got on her nerves, because it wasn't exactly what you would expect to hear on a palm-fringed beach. But when Arthur started to sing about God being a faithful father who cared for each one of his precious children, she had had enough. "For goodness sake, Arthur!" she spat out. "Do you have to sing such rubbish? If God cares for his children that much, why isn't he looking after us a bit better?"

Arthur laughed merrily. "Well, Maria, the Bible says that everything works for the good of those who love God

– even what seems to be really dreadful at the time is teaching us something, so we can't lose!" He laughed again. It was a confident laugh, a victorious laugh. You'd think he'd just won a medal, Maria glowered to herself, not been left homeless, destitute and soaking wet with an impossibly difficult journey ahead and the threat of imminent war. But she kept her thoughts to herself and gritted her teeth when he began to sing again with gusto – an incomprehensible new song this time about chains breaking off and going to "pastures new". He sang the same few lines over and over again, then, to Maria's immense chagrin, Emily joined in and Arthur gave her cheerful encouragement. How could she? thought Maria in disgust. Studiously ignoring her companions, Maria forced herself back to her tropical paradise as often as her anxious mind would allow.

It was still early when the little group arrived in Tonsfield, a drab-looking village, spread untidily along the main road. Nobody was about, but Maria had the feeling of being watched, which made her skin creep. They did hear the high-pitched sound of a chainsaw.

"They must have electricity here," remarked Emily.

"Chainsaws run on petrol," Maria corrected her. "Someone's probably chopping down trees for fuel." That was a weird thought.

They kept cycling, though Arthur and Emily no longer sang. Rufus ran around, wagging his tail. Having had a good night's sleep, meat for breakfast and plenty to drink from puddles along the way, he seemed to think the exercise a great idea.

The cyclists stopped when they reached what used to be a parade of shops. By the look of it there had been a newsagent, a small supermarket, a video hire place and a fish and chip shop, but now they were all boarded up. Rubbish blew about in the breeze and the sickening odour of rotting fish polluted the air. Not a soul was about. Several cars parked alongside had been looted and abandoned. It was eerie and disheartening.

"Let's look round the back," suggested Maria. "It stinks here." She wheeled her bike round the corner, followed by the others, but to her dismay a new, high wooden fence ran round the back of the shops with white paint scrawled on a padlocked gate saying "Private Property – Keep Out".

"I don't believe this," muttered Maria. "There must be some way in."

"What's the point," sighed Emily despondently, then sneezed. "There probably isn't any food left, anyway. And none of the shops sold clothes, even if we did have any money." The girls looked at each other hopelessly.

"Let's see if we can find a church," suggested Arthur. "There must be one in the village somewhere. There might be a group of Christians – if there is, they'll help us, I know they will."

"I'm going to get in here!" said Maria determinedly and, leaning her bike against the fence, she attempted to climb the gate. An immediate loud barking preceded the appearance of a large, bald man's head out of a first-floor window.

"Oi, you, what do you think you're doing?" he shouted roughly.

"We just want some food and clothes!" yelled back Maria boldly, though her heart was racing.

"You get out of 'ere!" the man yelled back. "We ain't got nothing for the likes of you!" The children looked at each other. "Go on, 'op it," shouted the man, "or I'll set my dogs on you!" He looked as if he meant it and the barking from behind him proved that he had the means to carry out his threat.

"Come on, Maria," said Emily urgently as Rufus returned the unfriendly barks, but Maria didn't need any urging. They cycled back to the main road and on through the village, hoping to see something else, anything else, that might help them. But almost before they knew it they had reached the last few houses. The little group stopped and looked at the country road stretching emptily away into the distance. Maria felt desperate.

"I didn't see a church, did you?" asked Arthur.

"No," answered Maria wretchedly. Emily sniffed and coughed. She was shaking with the cold.

"Maybe there isn't one."

"Must be!" countered Arthur. "This is England!"

Maria licked her dry lips, but still she hesitated. "It might take us ages to find it."

Arthur grinned. "What, in this tiny village? I tell you what, I'll go and look round – you two wait here and I'll come back and let you know. What do you think?"

"Please, Maria, say yes," begged Emily.

Maria was surprised at the strength of her plea. "But they'll be strangers!"

"Well, if they're Christians, they're my family at least!"

said Arthur, grinning as usual. "The family of God!" Maria did not have the energy to fight.

"OK," she shrugged. "We'll wait here."

Arthur was only gone five minutes, but even in that short time it felt funny without him. It was like he belonged with them, decided Maria, crazy though he was. He could be extremely irritating at times, yet his presence was reassuring. It was funny how someone could get on your nerves so much, but you liked them really, she reflected. It was like Mum and Dad and even Emily. She had thought that she hated them; it was only now that she realised that actually, she really did like them, sort of. It was weird.

Maria was relieved to see Arthur cycling back at a sprint. He was waving something in the air and he looked excited. Her hopes rose. "I found the church!" he yelled, as soon as he was within shouting distance. "There wasn't anybody there," he added, panting, as he reached his companions. "It was locked, but look what I found! A Bible! There was a whole stack of them in the porch!" His face was shining with triumph.

Maria stared at him. "Well, that won't taste very nice!" she said icily. This guy had two sides and one was raving loony. Here they were, wet through, hungry, thirsty and cold and he was excited about finding a book – and not just any old book – a dusty, musty, ancient old Bible! It was beyond comprehension. He didn't seem to be putting it on, either. She gave up.

"Shall we get moving then? It's cold, standing still." Maria could not remember ever feeling so despondent;

being banned from the school skiing trip paled into insignificance. That seemed like a lifetime ago, anyway. Arthur sang, if anything, more cheerfully than before, holding on to his precious bible with one hand as he cycled. Some of the songs were really weird, too and full of hallelujahs. One was about washing in the blood of a lamb. How disgusting could you get? Maria cycled ahead and ignored him. She didn't want to think about blood.

The road seemed endless. The landscape was flat, the sky was filled with dirty grey clouds that looked like torn bits of rag and Emily was coughing more and more. Maria tried to calculate in her head how long it would take them to get to the cottage, but gave up. If they carried on like this, they would be drinking from puddles and would end up with some disease and die before they got there anyway, so what was the point? She tried to have a conversation with her darling Adam but it didn't work, he was just too far away. At least her clothes were drying off a bit.

After a few miles, they saw a man working in a field with a horse. Maria stared in disbelief. This was worse than chopping down wood for fuel with a chainsaw – this was like returning to the Middle Ages! She started to wonder how long it would be before life returned to normal. Suppose it was several months, or even years . . . What if all the shops ran out of food and the farms and factories weren't working to stock them up? What if people couldn't get their money out of the banks? What would her family do if the insurance company never paid out for their stolen stuff? They would be penniless – they could even starve to death! And what if she couldn't go back to school? A few days ago she would have cheered, but now Maria started to wonder. What if she couldn't take her exams? She needed good marks to fulfil her ambition of becoming a pilot. But would there still be aeroplanes? And did she still want to be a pilot? Her thoughts rolled round and round, like the wheels of her bike.

At last, around midday, when the clouds parted to reveal a glimpse of warm, silvery sunshine, Maria noticed something different from the endless fields and hedgerows a little further on. A high, neat row of dark green conifer trees stood behind a large wooden sign. And behind them she could make out a building. Her heart gave a leap. Could it be a shop of some sort?

nineteen

"What does that sign say?" Maria wondered aloud. Arthur stopped singing and squinted at the board.

"Something for sale, maybe?" he ventured. Emily stared.

"It could be a garden centre," she guessed. Maria's spirits rose.

"I bet it is! And I bet there are chocolate bars by the checkouts!"

"And there will be water to drink at least!" Arthur whooped. "Yes, thank you, Lord! I'll beat you there, girls!"

Maria objected to being labelled "girls" with Emily, so she didn't rush. She joined the others in the paved area outside the shop, where terracotta pots, hanging baskets and tubs of golden daffodils decorated the entrance. Maria was startled at how white Emily looked after the short sprint and how heavily she was breathing. She was coughing badly, too. Surely she wasn't going to be ill? Maria's immediate reaction was anger. Why did Emily always have to ruin everything? Then, as her sister slumped wearily over her bike, Maria discovered with surprise a sudden caring she had not known possible. She needed to get Emily some warm clothes, something to eat and drink.

Arthur had not noticed anything amiss. "Look at this place!" he breathed. It was indeed a vast complex. All around, signs advertised areas of trees for sale, shrubs, fencing, water features and many other garden wares. An enormous glass-fronted store stood in front of them and to the right was a smaller, wooden building bearing the legend "fish". It all looked completely deserted.

Leaving their bikes by a display of cheerfully nodding daffodils, the three followed the path to the front entrance of the store and peered through the glass, while Rufus took a long drink from a fishpond. The store was enormous. And not only was it huge, it had diversified. Maria's eyes soaked up the goods with glee. "Clothes!" she yelled. "Look at those jackets, jeans, trainers . . . we've got to get in here!" Catching her reflection in the glass, she stared at her wild hair. Maybe there would be hairbrushes, too. Maybe she could even wash her hair.

"Aladdin's cave," breathed Emily, pressing her face against the window-pane. Her voice sounded nasal and she sneezed, several times in a row, then coughed again. Maria looked at her sister. She had to do something, fast; Emily couldn't be ill. Something else was on her mind, too.

"Are you going to come in?" she asked Arthur, combing her hair down with her fingers. "After all, it's closed." She spoke firmly. She didn't want him to have a go at her, accusing her of theft, because she fully intended to help herself to everything she wanted. Arthur appeared to be struggling with his conscience.

"I suppose I could take what I need, write it all down and send the money later," he reflected.

"Fine," replied Maria. "Do what you like, but me and Emily are just going to help ourselves, aren't we, Em?" Emily nodded listlessly, yawned then coughed again. She was shivering and her teeth chattered. Arthur raised his eyebrows in a concerned look at Maria and she grimaced back. "You stay here with Emily, I'll go and look round," she ordered him. She could do without him cramping her style. "I'll take Rufus with me." Arthur nodded.

"Sure."

Maria ran round the main building as quickly as she could, searching for a way to get in, Rufus at her heels. She gritted her teeth in determination. She would get in! There must be food here, even if it was only in a staff canteen. And she had seen warm, dry clothes – maybe she could find a toothbrush, too . . .

The only door round the back of the building was a fire door, but two little misted windows, close together about two metres up, looked like a possible way in. Toilet windows, probably, but beggars couldn't be choosers, Maria reminded herself. Good thing she was small! Otherwise it would have to be the front entrance, but that could be seen from the road and the glass was probably toughened anyway. There were pebbles and stones all round. Maria found a good heavy one and took aim at one of the little windows. She missed, but her second shot sent the glass tinkling down in a satisfying clatter. Ladies or gents? she wondered to herself with a grin. Rufus barked. "Shhh!" whispered Maria, hugging him in triumph and looking round, but the only people who came running were Arthur and Emily.

"I've smashed the window!" she crowed. The others just looked, Emily blankly, Arthur in consternation.

"You're not going to get in there, surely?" he asked.

"Just watch me!" Arthur opened his hands in a gesture of despair, but Maria was off, looking for a ladder, of which there were plenty to choose from. Nothing was going to put her off. She made a face at a CCTV camera with no tell-tale red light. "You're not working!" she jeered at it.

It was a cinch getting in through the window. Arthur held the ladder. All she had to do was to put her hand in through the broken pane of glass and open the catch. Climbing in was a bit of a squeeze; once her top half was in she had to hold on to the top of one of the cubicles in order to ease in her bottom half, but in a few seconds she had swung herself down on to a toilet and from thence on to the floor.

"I'll meet you round the front!" Maria shouted to the others, discovering with a grin that she was in the gents', but once out of the toilets she saw the fire door. She tried it. With one huge push on the bar it swung open. Her second break-in; another success! Maria was jubilant, but the others were more subdued. Only Rufus approved; he ran in with his tail wagging and started sniffing happily around. His toenails clicked and slid on the slippery floor, which was comical to watch, but Maria was the only one to laugh.

"I need a drink," said Emily weakly, sinking on to a padded garden chair. She closed her eyes. Maria glared at her. Why did everyone have to spoil her fun?

"What's your problem?"

"I'm tired. And I don't feel very well." Emily's voice was weak and she coughed pathetically.

Maria fought with herself. "We're all tired!" she spat out, but inside she was disturbed. Arthur was unsmilingly silent. He ought to be more grateful, too, thought Maria darkly. She gritted her teeth and ran to find something to eat and drink.

Just looking round the shop cheered her up. It was more like a department store than a garden centre and to think that she didn't need money, she could just walk round and take whatever she wanted – this was going to be serious fun! There were whole sections full of hideous and useless things; garden ornaments, gnomes with red, yellow and blue hats, vases, toys, cheap gifts and gaudy plastic flowers, but Maria grinned excitedly as she skipped past rows of designer clothes and footwear, gift-wrapped toiletries, cushions and brightly coloured throws. Sadly, she would not be able to take everything she liked, but she intended to pick out some decent clothes and stuff her panniers full. She was going to shop till she dropped! Yes! Determined to explore properly as soon as she had found breakfast, Maria made her way towards the tills, but round a stand of pot plants she made the best discovery yet. A café!

Maria stared greedily at the glass counter. Sandwiches and slices of gateaux were laid out neatly on clean white plates; underneath were little desserts in glass bowls and, joy oh joy, there was a huge fridge full of canned and bottled drinks – an oasis in the desert! "I've found a café!" she yelled to the others. Rufus nosed his way in to a plate of ham sandwiches and Maria helped herself to a large coke and ripped open a packet of cookies from a selection in a wicker basket near the till. Food, at last!

On closer inspection, most of the food on display looked decidedly past its best, but there were still plenty of other goodies to choose from. Running through to a little storeroom round the back, Maria gasped in astonished pleasure as she discovered cardboard boxes full of muffins, pies, cookies, crisps, flapjacks, chocolate biscuits, bread rolls and individual pots of jam, butter, milk and sugar. This was better than good; this was fantastic! Grabbing several large cellophane-wrapped chocolate muffins and an armful of cartons of orange juice she ran excitedly back to the others. Later, she promised herself, she would return for a serious pig-out!

"Here you go, guys, start on these," she announced excitedly to Emily and Arthur, dumping the armful of goodies on a nearby patio table, her eyes gleaming with the surprise. "Grab a chair! There's tons of stuff in the café and loads of decent clothes!" Arthur barely nodded and Emily glanced at Maria's treasure without enthusiasm, then closed her eyes.

"I'll just have a drink. Then could you get some clothes for me, Maria, please?" Emily leaned back and closed her eyes. "I'm cold." Arthur had found some fleece throws for her, but she still had her wet things on underneath and her teeth were chattering. Then she coughed again. It was a nasty, rasping cough that shook her whole body. Maria's cheerful mood evaporated. Suppose Emily was really ill? What would they do if she couldn't cycle any further?

twenty

Emily was asleep on a sunbed wearing warm, dry clothes, Rufus at her feet, when Maria and Arthur held council later. Arthur had lit a patio heater and he and Maria sat round it on gloriously soft reclining chairs, luxuriating in the warmth, easing their aching bodies and discussing their predicament.

Arthur looked a completely different person in blue jeans and a black fleece jacket. His school suit and the old man's jumper had done nothing for his image; now he looked decidedly more normal, approved Maria, adding to the stack of empty juice cartons and cellophane wrappers on the table. He was turning into a good friend. One you could trust, not like her last pig of a boyfriend, who had gone off on holiday and found someone else. Arthur would help her to take care of Emily, decide what to do.

However, despite the change of clothes, it was the same old Arthur. "I don't feel comfortable here, Maria," he told her as they munched their way through bags of crisps, apple pies and cherry almond cookies. "I don't mind admitting it. I know you don't think much of my relationship with God, but honestly, it's the most important thing in the world to me and I don't feel right about being here."

Maria stared at him. "What about Emily? We can't just drag her out now – look at the state of her!"

"Well, she's obviously exhausted. It hasn't been an easy few days for her, has it?"

"Are you blaming me?"

"Of course not! You are so . . . so prickly, Maria!" he grinned. Maria ignored him. She had enough on her mind. "Seriously, though," he continued, "she does need time to recover. Have a good sleep at least. But I'm not going to stay here. Sorry, but I'm going to leave as soon as possible."

Maria shrugged. "I think it's a great place. It's got everything we need."

"You would! My morals are different from yours!" Maria was just about to give a sarcastic reply when a sudden thought hit her like a medicine ball in the pit of her stomach. "Are you saying that you're going to push off and leave me and Emily here?"

Arthur laughed. "That thought had crossed my mind!" he admitted. "Bad company ruins good morals, that's what the Bible says."

Maria breathed in sharply. "Are you suggesting that me and Emily are bad company?" She couldn't believe it! The cheek of the lad!

Arthur laughed again. "You realise that you could get me arrested for helping you to break into this place? I held the ladder for you to get through the window and I walked in when you opened the fire escape. Plus," he added, eyes twinkling, "if it wasn't for meeting you, I'd probably be a lot nearer Dover by now!"

Maria was stunned. "I don't believe I'm hearing this!" Not only was he laughing at her, he had the audacity to blame her for his own lack of progress. She stood up, fuming. How dare he! "Go then!" she told him angrily. "We're obviously not good enough for you! Don't worry about us! Don't worry about Emily being ill – just go!"

"Maria, Maria," protested Arthur, holding up his hands. "That's not what I meant! No need to get angry . . ." Too late. Maria was livid.

"No need to get angry?" she shouted, standing up. "I knew this would happen! I just knew it! I said, 'Don't come in if you don't want to', but what do you do? Wait for me to do all the dirty work, then sit there, stuffing your face with the food I found and wearing the clothes that if I hadn't got in through the window you wouldn't be wearing! You ought to be grateful for what I've done, not sitting there calmly slagging me off as if I was some sort of major criminal!"

"Maria, shhh . . ." began Arthur, indicating Emily's sleeping form, but Maria was well into her tirade now.

"And what about us having to put up with all your rubbish songs? Washing in lamb's blood – what sort of nice religion is that? Well, we can do without you, Mr Religious who thinks he's better than everybody else! Get out, go on, go!" She stormed over to the fire exit and shoved the bar downwards with furious energy. The door burst open with a loud crash. Emily and Rufus woke up and stared. Maria stood there, eyes blazing, hands on her hips. "OUT!" she yelled at Arthur. Had he been a bit smaller, she would have hit him. She glared in his direction, but to her consternation, his eyes were twinkling and his bottom lip was trembling. Then he let out the most uproarious laugh.

"Sorry," he said, trying to straighten his face, but not succeeding. "I didn't mean to laugh, but . . ." and he nearly fell off his chair as he burst into another uncontrollable fit of laughter.

Maria gritted her teeth and stared at him grimly. What was funny? She didn't see anything to laugh at. Seeing a stand of cushions, she grabbed one off a shelf, stalked over and whacked him with it as hard as she could. "Get out!" she shouted again, seething with rage. Still laughing, he stood up and tried to grab it.

"No, Maria, no, you don't understand . . ." he tried, but she hit him again and again until he had recovered a little composure and grabbed it off her. Wiping tears of laughter from his eyes, he held her wrist.

"Let go of me!" she screamed.

"Not till you'll listen to me!"

"Listen to you? Never!" Maria furiously tried to grab back the cushion. Arthur was too strong for her, but he let her go and she ran to get another one. She chose a small, hard, leather one. This time, Arthur hit back.

"I was only joking," he said, parrying her blows and managing to get his own shots in between. "I didn't mean I was better than you!"

"What did you mean then, Mr Slippery!" shouted Maria, starting to enjoy herself. "Go on, then, say what you did mean!"

"I meant it would be better to find somewhere else to

stay for a while – but I meant all together, in a church hall or something, where it wouldn't be against the law."

"Rubbish! You're just trying to get out of it!" Her last words were muffled as Arthur's cushion got her in the face. Her words were tough, but she was relieved. Maybe he hadn't intended to leave them.

"Believe me, it's the truth! Maybe I could have got a bit further without you, but I was just pulling your leg about the morals. I'm enjoying your company too much to leave you!" Despite herself, Maria couldn't help smiling. This guy could be quite cute at times!

"What are you doing?" called Emily weakly from her sunbed. "Could someone close the door? It's cold." Arthur turned round and with split second timing Maria caught him off guard. With a big blow he staggered back, tripped over one of the table legs and landed sprawling on the shiny floor. Before he had time to recover himself, Maria put her foot on his chest and stood triumphantly over him.

"I win!" she glinted down at him, trying not to grin. "Apologise!"

"My most humblest of apologies, Ma'am," grovelled Arthur. "I appear to have said something which upset Ma'am, although it was only meant in jest and I wish to set the misunderstanding straight and say that I think Ma'am is a wonderful, courageous person."

"You're just saying that!"

"Who, me?" Arthur feigned innocence.

"Prove it by kissing my feet!" she demanded.

"What, in those disgusting trainers? No way!"

"I said, kiss my feet!"

"Oh no, anything but that!" He looked so silly, lying there on the floor. She laughed.

"I'll set Rufus on you!" Rufus looked lazily up from his bed on hearing his name, then tucked his head back down.

"Wow, I'm so scared!"

This time even Maria grinned. "OK, I'll let you off," she conceded and removed her foot.

After eating and drinking until just the thought of another cookie made her feel ill, Maria found two large backpacks for herself and Emily and stuffed both them and the bicycle panniers full of spare clothes, toiletries, the thickest throws she could find in place of sleeping bags, a torch each and stacks of food and drinks. Sadly, there weren't any maps, but aiming for the coast couldn't be that difficult; they would be sticking to the main road. The only thing seriously lacking was dog food, but fortunately Rufus seemed happy to eat anything. Anyway, it would only be for one more day, hopefully, Maria told herself. What would happen after that, she didn't dare even to consider.

Arthur took the bare minimum of everything and left a note on the checkout with his parents' address, then he watched over Emily while she slept, reading his battered Bible. He said he would pray for her, too. Maria laughed at him, but he just grinned back.

However, Maria was hugely relieved when Emily woke up after a couple of hours' sleep, feeling a bit better. Arthur made a big fuss of her, but Emily was embarrassed at all the attention and although she definitely had a nasty cough, she was just as keen as the others to get moving.

They left the garden centre after a last meal. Maria was sad to leave, in a way. Of course they had to get to the cottage, but it would have been a laugh to stay there for a night. Admittedly there was no running water, but that was probably the same everywhere now and there was heating, loads to eat and drink, luxurious sunbeds and hammocks to sleep on and Maria had almost managed to forget her troubles there for a little while, while she had "shopped". She had even caught herself humming as she chose a cute little teddy for Emily from a rack of cuddly toys. She wondered as she rifled through the rows of jackets, searching for the best labels and warmest designs, why she used to hate her sister so much. It was true that she was annoying sometimes, but so were Michelle and Trudi. Maybe it was because she had never really got to know her. It was obvious that their parents preferred her, but that was hardly Emily's fault, was it?

As the little party set off in the weakening afternoon sun, Maria's thoughts kept turning back to her parents and grandparents. She imagined them anxiously searching for them, not knowing for certain if she and Emily were still alive. She wouldn't entertain the thought that any of them might not be. Or the thought that a war could start at any time. But both stayed with her, somewhere deep down.

twenty-one

"We'll cycle as far as Emily and Rufus can manage," Maria said quietly to Arthur, as they rejoined the road.

Arthur nodded. "Good idea. We'd better not push her though." Arthur had taken Emily's panniers to spare her the load, but still, progress was slow. Rufus was brilliant on the whole, but every so often they had to stop and wait for him while he sniffed about and Emily had to get off and push her bike up the slightest hill. However, little by little, the number of miles to Dover decreased. Every signpost brought fresh hope, fresh jubilation and the pedals turned faster for a while: "28 miles", "27", then after a long straight stretch and a gentle downwards slope, "25".

To pass the time, they told jokes. Arthur knew the most and the worst. Emily coughed every time she laughed, but apart from that they could have been just out for a bike ride, thought Maria, like they used to with their parents when they were little, going home to buttered crumpets and chocolate cake.

When they had run out of jokes, Arthur started to sing again; Emily tried to join in, but it made her cough worse, so she gave up. While Arthur sang, Maria and Emily had a civilised conversation; the first that Maria could ever remember.

"Thanks for the clothes," Emily said to Maria. "I really like this jacket. And my teddy, he's really cute."

"That's OK," replied Maria generously. "I didn't pay for them!" They both laughed. Emily pulled the little bear that Maria had chosen for her out of her pocket and tucked him in the front of her new padded jacket, as if he were looking out. He wasn't very big, but he had a cute face and was made of the softest, creamiest fur, with chocolate brown paws and ears.

"I had to leave Doggus in that cottage." Emily sounded matter-of-fact, but Maria didn't know what to say. Doggus was Emily's oldest, favourite cuddly toy dog. He was nearly threadbare, because she had had him since she was little. Maria used to torment her sister mercilessly about her baby toy, but now Doggus had gone. Maria had lost lots of things herself; her mobile phone, her telly, her computer and all her CDs, but Doggus was irreplaceable. She didn't know what to say.

"I didn't know you'd brought him," she managed eventually. "Maybe we'll be able to get him back, later on." But she knew it was impossible. And she knew that Emily knew it too.

"Maybe. Anyway, now I've got a new teddy and a real dog!" She smiled as she stroked the little bear and looked fondly towards Rufus, who rewarded her with a tail wag, but she was blinking back tears. Maria looked away.

Crossing over the motorway bridge was another milestone. They had heard the noise of engines and horns for a while, so they knew it was coming up, but even so, it was quite an eye-opener. An unbelievable assortment of abandoned lorries, vans, cars and every type of vehicle in between, some whole, some nearly in one piece, some almost smashed to a pulp, lay in all sort of positions, all over both sides of the carriageway, as far as they could see. The few vehicles that were still moving towards Dover were picking their way through the debris. Nothing was moving in the direction of London. It looked like a disaster movie. Nobody made any comment. They all just kept cycling.

The next big event was joining the old main London/Cartford road. The traffic was fairly heavy here, which brought a surreal normality to everything. Fortunately, Rufus was very good about keeping to the grass verges. In the warm spring sunshine, with cars, vans, motorbikes and even lorries whizzing by, it was easy to ignore the smashed and looted vehicles, petrol stations and eating places that they passed. Maria wondered why so many people were on the move. Maybe the threat of war was over . . . or maybe it was imminent. She shrugged to herself and tried not to think about it. She tried not to listen to Emily's cough, either. It seemed to be getting worse. But maybe, if they could keep going, they could even make it home tonight, after all . . .

Pleased with their progress, it was an aching but reasonably cheerful party that made a stop for a snack and a rest in a lay-by, which they shared with a supermarket lorry. There were no benches and the grass was still damp from the morning's rain, so they sat on the kerb. Courtesy of the garden centre, the little group tucked into crisps, flapjacks and chocolate biscuits, washed down with cans of coke and lemonade.

"I'm sick of cold food and drinks," sighed Maria, pouring a bottle of mineral water into a plastic bowl for Rufus. "I could murder a cup of tea and a roast dinner. Steaming hot. Or a really hot chicken tikka masala, followed by hot fudge cake with loads of hot chocolate sauce!"

"Mmm," agreed Emily, a far away look in her eyes.

"You just ought to be grateful . . ." began Arthur, then he caught Maria's eye. "OK, OK," he backed down, grinning, "I'll just be grateful myself!"

Maria grinned back. "You're getting to know me!"

"Where are we going to stay tonight?" asked Emily. "It's starting to get dark." There was a pause.

"What do you want to do?" Arthur asked her.

"I don't mind," said Emily, looking surprised to be asked. Maria looked round at her companions hopefully.

"I know it's a long way, but do you think we could make it to the coast tonight? Even if it's really late when we get there, it's got to be better than staying out here."

Arthur looked at Emily as a fit of coughing shook her whole body.

"Listen, Cartford's not far off," he replied. "We could look for a church or a community centre or something like that to stay in."

Maria shook her head. "That means going out of our way. Anyway, I don't like the thought of being with a load of adults. They'd tell us what to do. I can do without interfering old cronies poking their noses into our business." Arthur laughed aloud. Emily didn't.

"I think it's a good idea of Arthur's. How far's Cartford?"

"Two miles, by the last signpost," Maria informed her. "We do want to stay on the main road, though, don't we? In case someone's looking for us?"

Emily thought for a minute. "I see what you mean – about the main road. OK then," she agreed, although her face shone even paler than usual in the fast-retreating light.

"I don't think we'll make it to the coast tonight," admitted Arthur. Looking apologetically at Maria, he quietly nodded towards Emily. "It's still an awfully long way."

Maria pursed her lips. She didn't want it to be too far. Maybe they could still do it. Surprise themselves. "How about we just keep going then, and see what turns up?" she suggested.

"Even if it's a barn?" joked Arthur. Maria made a face and chucked an empty juice carton in his direction.

Just as they were packing up to leave, Maria was startled to hear a cab door slam. Turning round, she saw a man sauntering away from the supermarket lorry towards them.

"Hi there!" the man saluted them, with what seemed to Maria like a false smile. "You kids OK?" He was a small, white man with greying hair and a scruffy beard, dressed in faded blue denim jeans and jacket. Rufus' hackles rose and he growled at the man, who glanced at him, then ignored him.

"Fine, thanks," Emily replied, coughing.

"Great!" said Arthur, collecting up the rubbish.

Maria stared suspiciously. "What's it to you?"

"Just wanted to make sure you're OK," shrugged the man, eyeing their laden bikes and designer clothes. "You cycling somewhere on your own?"

"What does it look like?" asked Maria. She got up to go. Why did he want to know? He laughed, but it sounded kind of hollow.

"You obviously haven't been listening to the news. It's dangerous out here on the roads after dark. Lonely. Things can happen." He sounded menacing, but as he backed off towards the lorry, he was still smiling. "Don't worry, I'm not hassling you or anything, just thought you might like a lift somewhere . . . but you obviously don't!" Maria narrowed her eyes at him.

"Obviously!" she said sweetly and deliberately looked in the opposite direction in a gesture of dismissal.

"Where are *you* going?" Emily asked the man quickly. Maria turned and glared at her sister.

"Well, where are you going? Dover?" the man guessed. Emily nodded before Maria could stop her.

"It's none of your business," snapped Maria, glaring at the man, then grabbed Emily and turned to leave. "If you don't go I'll set my dog on you!" she warned him. Rufus barked obligingly.

"OK, OK," the man said, lifting his hands. "No need to get nasty! Just wanted to help, that's all. You'll regret not taking up my offer, though, I promise you that." His last words sounded like a threat, but they ignored him as he turned round and walked back to the lorry.

"Come on," Maria said to the others, as the cab door slammed, "time to go." Arthur was ready. "You stupid fool!" Maria hissed at Emily. "Don't you remember what Mummy always told you – don't talk to strangers? I can't believe you told that man where we're going!"

Emily had tears in her eyes. "I didn't, not really. But suppose he was going near Callum? We could have had a lift – we'd be there in like, an hour . . . and he said it was dangerous out here in the dark and it'll be dark soon!" Emily started to sniff and Maria saw her tears falling, but she was still cross. What did that man mean, they would regret not taking up his offer? They passed the lorry. There were two men in the cab, smoking, following them with their eyes. Maria was disturbed.

"Look at them, they're not going anywhere! That man just wanted to find out where we were going, didn't he Arthur? Him and his mate – they're probably just common thieves! Suppose we got in his lorry? They'd probably nick all our stuff and dump us somewhere with nothing! Or kill us and dump our bodies . . ."

Arthur gave a warning look at Maria, as if to say, don't worry Emily, keep it between ourselves. "Well, we'll never know now!" he said lightly, though Maria could tell that he was concerned, too. Arthur did not often look serious. She felt like screaming.

As the sun started to dip the traffic eased off, then ceased altogether. Maria felt small and increasingly vulnerable. Why had everybody left the road? It was still only early evening. Surely some people must still be coming home from work? Admittedly, the power still seemed to be off – no lights were lit anywhere – but wasn't anybody going out, or going home from somewhere? The words of the man from the lorry went round and round in Maria's mind. "It's dangerous on the road after dark", "Things can happen." What did everyone else know that she didn't? It was weird and most discomfiting. It was hard, too, admitting that nobody had found them yet. What could have happened to Mum and Dad, Granny and Grandpa? Why hadn't they come? Had they run out of petrol? Or had they just given up? Maybe they were ill or even . . .

As night deepened, Maria began to change her mind about going as far as they could that night and joined Arthur in looking for somewhere they could stay. It was no big deal, she tried to persuade herself; they would still get to the cottage tomorrow. It wasn't the distance that bothered her; it was the all-pervading darkness descending upon her, from which she felt the need to hide. It seemed to be laughing at her, glad that she was out and in its power. It seemed to be only waiting for the last rays of light to be extinguished so that it could get her. It was already working on her hope, sowing dread in its place, enjoying her fear. Maria's heart raced as she kept looking round, waiting for something awful to happen.

After a while, it did. As the group cycled slowly along an empty stretch of dual carriageway between two roundabouts, the stillness was shattered by the sound of a car approaching at break-neck speed behind them. Looking behind her, Maria saw a bright yellow car, lights blazing, engine roaring and tyres screeching.

"Get off the road!" yelled Maria. Everyone made a dash for the grass verge and sat on their bikes, waiting for the car to pass. Rufus ran up the slope, barking. The roaring engine came closer. Maria turned to look. The car, filled with lads jeering out of the windows and waving beer bottles, was heading straight for her.

twenty-two

The thunder of the car's engine drowned out Rufus' barking. Maria didn't have time to move. She could hear the lads shouting inexplicably "ONE, ONE, ONE, ONE," as she closed her eyes and braced herself, waiting to feel the crunch as the car smashed into her, but all it did was clip the rear end of her bike as it swept past, the engine squealing as the tyres struggled to keep a grip on the muddy verge. Maria wobbled and toppled over, her bike landing on top of her as the lads in the car cheered triumphantly, jeered at the cyclists, then began to yell "TWO, TWO, TWO, TWO," as they roared away.

"Maria!" screamed Emily. She and Arthur came rushing to help her up and Rufus licked her face, but unbelievably, apart from feeling pretty shaken up, she and the bike were both unharmed.

"What do they think they're doing?" seethed Maria, brushing down her new jacket. "I thought they were going to smash right into me!"

"Don't worry, they've gone now," soothed Arthur, but he was wrong. At the roundabout, the car sped round in full circle and screeched back up the road on the other side of the carriageway. As they passed, Maria could hear them still yelling, "Two, two, two, two," in their direction, through the central reservation.

"They're going to come back!" screamed Emily in fright.

"They're going to hit us again!" cried Maria in shocked disbelief. "Three, four, five and six, probably, till we're all dead!"

"Turn off your lights!" yelled Arthur. "And get down to the roundabout! Take one of the side roads! Quick, before they see us!" The three of them, closely followed by Rufus, shot down to the roundabout as the car disappeared out of sight and they all followed Arthur up the first exit; a narrow, leafy lane. When they could go no further, they stopped, in the heavy shadows of the trees, panting desperately. They were just in time. Maria heard the car race back down the road and watched the yellow streak tear over the roundabout. If they had still been there, the car would have got them for sure and who knows if the ambulance service still existed? Just as likely, they would be left to bleed to death on the road. Maria shuddered. This was probably what the man from the lorry had meant. She looked grimly round at the others. Emily was coughing badly, doubled up. Thank goodness Arthur had the panniers, she thought, or Emily would never have made it. Arthur was frowning as he reached down to pat Rufus, who had sank down onto the road, panting.

"Thank God," sighed Arthur. "They've gone."

"Please don't come back," begged Maria under her breath, but her hopes were shattered as she heard the car return slowly to the roundabout and circle it menacingly, like a big cat sniffing out its prey.

Maria realised that she was shaking. Wildly, she looked round for somewhere to run to, but beyond the narrow avenue of trees and bushes was a barbed wire fence. She clenched her fists and closed her eyes in desperation as she heard Arthur praying out loud, "Please, Lord, send them away!" After a terrible, weird moment, when the only sound was a song thrush singing cheerfully, she heard the car burst to life and shoot off back the way it had come.

Maria let out her breath. "They've gone I think. For now." The roar of the car's engine faded into the distance. Tears sprung to Maria's eyes as she leaned her aching body over the handlebars of the bike and took a few deep breaths. How were they supposed to survive out here? Things were worse than she had thought. The whole country had gone mad. She remembered what she had said to Emily when they were crossing the bridge over the motorway near their home yesterday – if the police weren't working, anybody could do anything . . . she had been right, that was exactly what was happening. It was all a horrible, horrible nightmare.

"We should have taken that lift!" wailed Emily. "That man from the lorry was right – it is dangerous out here!"

Maria sat up. "I reckon that man sent them to get us!" she retorted hotly. "I reckon he was after our stuff. Didn't you see him eyeing it all up? That's what he meant when he said 'Things can happen'." Arthur said nothing. He and Maria looked at each other through the darkness. Maria tried to hide her mixture of despair and fear, but

Arthur seemed to sense it. The flapping of a wood pigeon's wings made Maria jump as she got out her torch from her backpack, wishing she still had the map she had torn from the atlas. She blinked her eyes furiously to clear her eyes of tears. Arthur cleared his throat.

"What do you want to do now?" he asked.

Maria paused, swallowing hard. "I think we should follow this road for tonight," she said eventually, trying to hide the shake in her voice. "We could find somewhere to stay – maybe in one of Arthur's barns or something, then come back to the main road again in the morning, when it's light. What do you think?"

"We've got to stay on the main road!" wailed Emily. "If we don't, Mum and Dad won't find us, you said so yourself!" Maria looked up, concerned. Emily was getting hysterical. She and Arthur exchanged a glance.

Arthur cleared his throat and spoke gently. "Emily, if your Mum was here . . ."

"She's not, though, is she?" interrupted Emily, sniffing, tears streaming down her face.

Arthur tried again.

"No, but if she was, she would say that the most important thing was for you to be safe, wouldn't she? I know my Mum would. The main road isn't very safe at the moment, with that crazy car about, but it looks better here. What do you think, Maria?"

Maria nodded. "We need somewhere to hide out till morning. We'll get back to the main road at first light, yeah?" She tried to sound hopeful, cheerful, though she felt nothing of the sort.

Emily carried on sobbing as she wiped her tears away with a shaking hand. "Couldn't we go back and try and find that lorry? That man might still give us a lift if we ask."

Arthur and Maria exchanged another glance. "I told you, I don't trust him," said Maria firmly. "Anyway, it's too far in the wrong direction."

"I agree," nodded Arthur.

"You two have just got suspicious minds," Emily shouted. "The man was just worried about us!" The shouting made her cough, terribly. Maria was disturbed. They had overdone it. They had pushed Emily too far. Rufus whined. Maria absent-mindedly gave him a pat and a cookie from her pocket.

"Let's vote on it," she suggested. "I vote we take this side road, just for tonight, and find somewhere to stop as soon as possible. Rufus is tired too." Arthur nodded in agreement. "Two against one," Maria shrugged. "Three if you count Rufus."

"That's so unfair," yelled Emily, her voice rising hysterically again. "Just because you're older than me, you think you know everything! And now we're going to miss Mum and Dad!" With that, she rode away up the dark lane, sobbing loudly.

"They won't come in the dark!" called Maria after her. "And we'll be back on the main road tomorrow!" But Emily didn't answer. She just started coughing again, so badly that she was nearly sick. Maria swallowed. They did not even know if their parents were still alive, she thought wearily, her stomach grinding. She felt sick herself. Sick in her stomach, sick in her heart. Arthur said nothing, but squeezed her arm as he joined her and they rode on in silence, side by side.

What was left of the coloured clouds sailed away with the last blush of the sun and the cold sky filled with stars. The avenue of trees that had lined the winding lane thinned out and mist began to gather in the fields. It got colder and colder. Only the moon was sympathetic. Whether they turned left or right along the winding lane it shone ahead, like a friendly presence, guiding them through the darkness.

Maria and Arthur kept their eyes open for somewhere to spend the night. After a couple of false hopes – a building that turned out to be a hen coop and a barn that was full of manure, the weary group arrived at the entrance to a National Heritage building. They all stopped. "Parlingworth House", announced the sign. Arthur grinned. "Would this be good enough for you ladies?" He pretended to doff his cap. Maria couldn't help smiling back. How did he manage to stay so cheerful? Emily seemed to be sulking. She just shrugged and looked away. She had not spoken since the incident with the car.

"Shall we give it a try, then?" asked Arthur.

Maria nodded wearily. The impressive wrought iron gates were open, as if welcoming them in. "Might as well."

On one side of the long, curving drive, sheep with their little lambs tore at the grass in the moonlight. On the other side, the silhouette of a horse stood proud against the dark sky. An owl hooted as the cyclists rode tiredly through the archway of the imposing gatehouse, as if announcing their arrival. The little group stopped and stared when they reached the other side. It was like going back in time. A beautiful, formal garden with clipped trees, statues and neat flowerbeds stretched out before them. Further ahead, up a flight of stone steps, stood the house, built of creamy stone, which gleamed luminously in the moonlight. "House" was hardly the word; even mansion hardly did the building justice. It was an impressive sight; enormous, majestic, with battlements, elaborate chimneys and hundreds of leaded windows, which seemed like eyes, looking at them as if in pleased surprise to have company.

"Wow, how about that!" breathed Arthur. The scene was only spoiled by ugly tyre marks scrawled over the lawns.

"Someone's already been here," remarked Maria nervously. She called Rufus to heel. Arthur cycled over to study the muddy tracks.

"It looks as if they've gone now, though," he said. Emily still said nothing. She looked down at her feet, sniffing and coughing.

"Are you sure they've gone?" asked Maria dubiously, staring at the windows of the house and melting into the shadows of the gatehouse. "If there's someone still here, we'd better be careful."

"Pretty sure," said Arthur. "Look, these are the coming tracks and these are the going ones. Two lots, by the look of it. What a mess they've made of the grass!"

"So, are we going in then?" asked Maria, hopefully.

"We can try!" replied Arthur. He approached a topiary

peacock and gave it a pat. "Look after this for me, old boy, would you?" he asked it and, leaving his bike leaning against the bird's leafy pedestal, he ran up the steps to the front door.

Maria didn't feel like laughing. "What are you going to do, knock?" she scoffed instead. Emily dumped her bike on the path and went and sat on a bench, coughing. Telling Rufus to stay with Emily, Maria left her own bike with Arthur's and ran up the steps to join him by the enormous oak door.

"We've got to get Emily somewhere to sleep," she whispered urgently.

Arthur nodded. "You stay with her. Give her something to eat and drink, tell her it'll be OK. I'll go and have a look round the back, see if there isn't an outhouse or something we can sleep in. I can't imagine actually getting in to the house – security's bound to be tight. But there must be old sheds or stables or something – might even have hay."

Maria nodded. "Ooh, hay, I can't wait!"

Arthur laughed. "So you have got a sense of humour!"

Maria made a face at him. "Be careful."

Arthur grinned. "I will. And don't you get into any more arguments!"

Maria grinned back. "Oh, shut up!"

"Where's Arthur going?" asked Emily, listlessly, as Maria joined her on the bench.

"Find us somewhere to sleep. Want something to eat while we're waiting? Pie, biscuits, crisps?" Emily shook her head and just stared ahead at nothing.

"I'm not hungry," she said weakly. "I think I've got a temperature. Sometimes I feel hot and sometimes I feel cold. And my chest hurts. Really badly." She coughed again and closed her eyes. Maria noticed two bright spots on Emily's normally pale cheeks. That was worrying. What were you supposed to do for someone who had a temperature? She tried to think straight. Fluids, she remembered her dad saying. That was it. Drinks.

"What about a drink? Orange juice, lemonade?" Emily made no reply; she just coughed and coughed until she doubled up. Then she closed her moist eyes.

"It hurts when I cough," she moaned. Maria felt the panic welling up inside. This was serious. They had to finish the journey tomorrow, they just had to! She ran back to her bike. "What are we going to do, Rufus?" she muttered anxiously, pulling a throw out of her bag. Running back to Emily, she wrapped it around her and looked anxiously round for Arthur.

"Thanks," Emily whispered, snuggling into the warmth of the fleece. Rufus licked her face and whined.

"Don't do that," muttered Maria. "You're frightening me." But that was nothing to the shock she had as she turned. The front door of the old building was opening, making a terrible creaking noise and a shadowy figure stood in the doorway.

"Hey! You!" shouted a deep voice in a foreign accent. "What are you doing on my land?"

twenty-three

Rufus ran up to the figure and pushed past him into the house. "Not so fast, Rufus," said a familiar voice. "Ladies first!" It was Arthur!

"If that's your idea of a joke, I don't think much of your sense of humour," snapped Maria as Arthur, laughing cheerfully, ran down the stone steps to her and Emily. "You stupid boy, you frightened me half to death! What a pathetic thing to do!" Her heart was still thumping from the shock. Emily sat up, yawned and coughed.

"I thought it was quite good!" replied Arthur. "I got you, didn't I? And guess what?"

"Just tell me, I'm not in the mood."

"The back door was open!" crowed Arthur delightedly. "I just pushed it and walked in! There's not much furniture left – that explains the tracks – removal vans, probably. But it'll be warmer inside than out here. We might even be able to light a fire! You should see the fireplaces!"

"Arthur, you were trespassing!" mocked Maria, feeling slightly less grumpy now that the fright was over, although she did not intend to let him get away lightly with scaring her like that. Arthur still grinned from ear to ear, looking decidedly pleased with himself.

"Don't be grouchy, Maria, it's National Heritage, public property and it's fantastic in there, come and see! I bet you've never slept anywhere like this before!" He grinned again and bowed, picking up his bag and ushering the girls in past him. As if he owned the place, thought Maria crossly, taking off her backpack. All he did was push a door open.

But soon Maria began to soften. It was an amazing place. The entrance hall alone was as big as last night's cottage. Maria smiled as she looked around, in spite of herself. When she was little she used to dress up in her mother's sequinned ball gowns and pretend that she lived in a place like this. Wood panelling covered the walls from floor to ceiling and an elegant, sweeping staircase curved round, as if inviting them upstairs. Flashing her torch upwards and around, Maria noticed an elaborately carved ceiling and a wonderful, huge chandelier, but there was no way she was going to let Arthur have the satisfaction of seeing that she liked it. "Bit ostentatious," she sniffed loftily. "But I suppose it will do for tonight."

"Are you kidding?" gasped Arthur. "It's fantastic! Look at the carving on that mantelpiece – look at the work in that coat of arms!"

"It's all right, I suppose. Prefer pine myself."

"You're joking!"

"Look, let's just get sorted – it's got a roof, that's all that matters. Are we going to bring the bikes in?"

Arthur grinned. "Better, I suppose. You never know." He did not elaborate, but Maria agreed. You never knew anything any more. They left Emily sitting on the staircase with Rufus and went to fetch the bikes.

"Emily's got a temperature," Maria told Arthur anxiously as soon as her sister was out of earshot. "She says she keeps going hot and cold and her cough's definitely getting worse. What are we going to do?"

Arthur stopped. "Look, I know everything seems to be against us," he said gently, "but it's going to be OK – believe me, Maria, I just know God is taking care of us. I believe he's sent angels to protect us – it happened to me once before, in my country, similar sort of circumstances. I can't see them, but . . . I can almost feel them." Angels! There it was again. Maria looked round, half-expecting to see something white with wings hovering around the bikes, but she quickly pulled herself together. What was she turning into? Some sort of religious freak? She gave Arthur the most withering look she could muster and walked on.

They hid the bikes in an empty room opposite the front door. "Shall we go straight upstairs?" asked Arthur, closing the door and indicating Emily, without her noticing, to Maria. "That's where the bedrooms will be."

"Well aren't we just so clever," said Maria sarcastically, elbowing him out of the way. "We know that bedrooms are upstairs!"

Arthur laughed. "Sorry! I don't know what came over me!"

The house was a veritable rabbit warren of passages, rooms and staircases. Maria secretly thrilled at the polished wooden floors, the spacious corridors, a gallery overlooking what probably used to be a banqueting hall and the beautiful leaded windows everywhere. Evidently much of the furniture, rugs, pictures and other antiques that used to be on display had recently been taken; marks on the floor and walls showed where different items had stood or hung and an expensive-looking painted vase lay smashed in many pieces on the floor by one of the window sills.

The largest pieces of furniture had been left, which fortunately included the beds. "Too heavy to move, probably," decided Arthur, giving one a hefty push that made no impression whatever. "I wonder if the rest of the stuff has been put into storage until all this is over?"

"Some crook's probably nicked the lot to sell," shrugged Maria, "but who cares? They're only boring old antiques. History's just a pointless waste of time."

"You don't really mean that?" asked Arthur incredulously.

"She does," replied Emily wearily, sinking on to the soft mattress of a four-poster bed, in what appeared to have been the lady of the manor's bedroom. Arthur shook his head.

"You never cease to amaze me, Maria," he grinned. Maria took it as a compliment and grinned back. Emily heaved herself right up on to the bed and closed her eyes.

The next room was probably the Lord's bedroom. It was bigger than the Lady's, but less feminine. This room was furnished with another lavish four-poster bed, intricately carved and embellished with a coat of arms.

"We'll camp here for tonight, shall we?" asked Arthur, noticing that they had left Emily behind. "You ladies can have the beds; I'll sleep on the dressing room floor."

Maria nodded and dumped the bags and panniers next to the marble hearth. "Suits me."

Leaving Emily to sleep and Rufus to keep guard, Arthur and Maria went off to check out the rest of the house. It was in the shape of a huge letter E. Maria inwardly thrilled at the size of the place, the number of rooms, the elegance of the carved wood and the solid, dependable cream stone. She lost count of the number of staircases. There were large rooms and small rooms, mostly empty, but all with a warm, gentle atmosphere; none were in the least bit ghostly, even by torchlight. The explorers paused in what must once have been a chapel. Its windows were of stained glass, depicting scenes from various Bible stories and at one end of the room was an altar. "Loads of people must have prayed here over the years," reflected Arthur, "and just think, through all the centuries, God hasn't changed a bit." For once Maria didn't have anything to say. The chapel seemed to be agreeing with him. There was the same serenity in that little room that Maria had felt outside her home, before she and Emily had left. She had almost forgotten what it had felt like. It was good. Really good. With her back to Arthur, she closed her eyes and soaked it up.

"Do you mind if I stay here on my own for a minute?" asked Arthur eventually.

Maria turned round and shrugged. "If you want." She leaned on a windowsill in the corridor while she waited for Arthur, staring out at the dark sky and the darker hills. The peace from the chapel stayed with her. Tonight she could almost believe that there really was a God caring for them, like Arthur said.

"Can I tell you about something?" Arthur asked Maria a little while later as they passed through a series of kitchen rooms towards the back door.

"Whether I say yes or no you probably will anyway."

Arthur laughed. "True! Listen, it's about the blood of the lamb, you know, the song I was singing earlier, that you didn't like?"

Maria was immediately suspicious. What was this leading to? She thought of the lambs that they had passed on the way in and wished that she had Rufus with her. "So?"

"The lamb is Jesus. You know he died on a cross?"

"What are you on about?"

"Did you ever study the Passover in Judaism?"

"Might have. What's that got to do with anything?"

"Well, Jesus gave up his life as a sacrifice, like the blood of the lamb did for the Jews at Passover, to separate them apart for God. You know, before the exodus from Egypt."

"So you're a Jew then?"

"No, Silly!"

Maria shook her head. This guy was crazy. "I don't know what you're on about."

"When I was singing about the blood of the lamb, I was singing about the sacrifice that Jesus made for me – and for everybody else. I deserve to die because I'm a sinner, but Jesus died in my place – that's the blood of the lamb bit. Now all those who believe in him and are born again can go to heaven – we've been forgiven and aren't separated from God by our sins any more."

"So what has that got to do with me?" At least he didn't mean real lambs.

"Maria, are you crazy? You shouldn't ignore God! After all, he loves you and wants to show you the way to heaven."

"You think you know everything, don't you, Arthur – even the way to heaven!" mocked Maria. She still understood nothing, but at least Arthur wasn't going to do any sacrificing himself.

"It's not me, it's in the Bible!"

"Yeah, yeah!" He might be talking rubbish, but at least it was innocuous rubbish. Laughing, they pulled open the heavy back door and found themselves in a courtyard surrounded by three outbuildings. Beyond these was a wooded area. The night was cold and still; their breath came in clouds of condensation, but the moon still shone down in friendly indulgence. Maria and Arthur grinned at each other and stepped out.

The nearest building was now a restaurant; next to that came the gift shop. Both were locked, but the door to the third and longest building was open; it was a stable door. Maria peered in. Although it was empty at the moment, three stalls still appeared to be in use; there was a faint smell of horses and leather. Obviously at some point in the history of the house there had been many horses here, but now, apart from the feed bins and tack room, most of the stables had been converted in to a museum of farm machinery.

"Shall we go back?" asked Arthur. A snort coming from

the direction of the nearest field made Maria turn in consternation, but she soon saw what was making the noise.

"Let's go and see the horses!" Her eyes shone in the darkness. Arthur nodded, grinning.

A rather tatty-looking chestnut mare stood alone in the field, munching grass. "Come on, girl!" called Maria, leaning over the gate and clicking her tongue, but the horse just raised her head for a moment, then carried on eating. Maria ran back to the stables. This time, seeing Maria carrying a feed bucket, the horse came straight to the gate.

"Look out!" called Arthur, backing up as the mare stuck her head over the gate. "Wow, I didn't realise horses were as big as this!"

Maria laughed at him. "Wimp!" she said, offering the mare a wrinkled apple. "Actually, this really is quite a big lady – sixteen or seventeen hands I should say. You're a beautiful girl, aren't you," she crooned, patting her neck. Clouds of dust rose. "She's been neglected," added Maria. "Maybe no one's been to see to her since Tuesday."

Arthur coughed. "True, it needs a bath! It's really muddy. And its tail looks like a collection of rats' tails!"

"Don't be rude! And she's not an 'it', she's a she. Aren't you, darling?" crooned Maria. Under the scruffy, neglected coat, Maria could see the mare was a quality horse and would be handsome if she were groomed and cared for. "All you need is a good groom, don't you?"

"She has got lovely eyes," admitted Arthur. "Look at her eyelashes! And she certainly likes those food things!" The mare snorted as she searched Maria's hands and jacket for something else to eat.

"They're called pony nuts!" laughed Maria, climbing the gate and jumping down into the field.

Arthur cautiously joined her and they stood there together for a few minutes, stroking and talking to their new friend in the moonlight. She lapped up the attention. "How could anyone believe that something as beautiful as this happened by accident?" asked Arthur admiringly. "She's just so perfect!"

"What accident?"

"You know, despite the evidence, some people still believe in evolution!" grinned Arthur. "You can see someone designed this horse – just look at her! People just don't want to admit there might be a creator, because they don't want to believe that there might be a God."

Maria didn't feel like getting into a pointless argument. "Where do you think the other horses are?" she asked. "There were three stalls." She scanned the field with her torch, to no avail. "Looks like someone's taken them. This one must be lonely."

"How do you know about horses?"

"I used to ride, when I was younger." Maria smiled to herself as she stroked the mare's velvety nose. "Even did some jumping. Got quite good, really – won a few prizes in shows. Then I got interested in other things – music, shopping, stuff like that. How about you?"

"I've never been this close to a horse before. I've never ridden. I'd like to, though."

"Really? Well, I'll teach you one day, if you like."

"Thanks!" grinned Arthur, patting the horse rather gingerly. "That would be brilliant!" Neither of them mentioned the fact that after tomorrow, they might never see each other again.

They stayed there for a while, enjoying the peace and the companionship. Only the gentle sound of the horse's warm breathing and her hooves on the damp earth disturbed the still night air. Neither of them wanted to leave. Eventually, Arthur broke the silence.

"Well, we'd better get a few hours sleep, don't you think?" Maria, yawning, but not moving, reluctantly nodded her agreement.

"I'll groom her in the morning, before we go." She leaned against the horse and gave her a last pat. "You're so gorgeous, aren't you?"

"Yes, I am," replied Arthur in a silly voice. Maria gave him a shove and they both laughed.

At that moment, the peaceful night was shattered by a far away high-pitched scream, followed by urgent barking. Both came from the direction of the house. Maria stiffened in fear. "Emily, Rufus!" she gasped as a chill ran down her spine. Then she started to run.

twenty-four

Maria had never moved so fast in her life, but even so she reached the bedrooms after Arthur, who was picking up a dazed Emily from the floor by the time she arrived.

"I fell out of bed," Emily whimpered. "It's so high up. Thank you, Arthur. We're still in that castle aren't we? I forgot where I was and it was dark." She closed her eyes. "My chest and my throat hurt so badly. Maria, don't leave me again. Are we going to die? I heard the planes come back." She doubled up as she coughed. "Ow!" she cried. "That hurts!" Beads of perspiration covered her forehead and tears dripped down her red cheeks.

"You were only dreaming about the planes," said Maria, still panting from the sudden exercise.

"You're just saying that," wailed Emily, tears dripping down her pale face.

"Of course I'm not!" retorted Maria. Anger began to take over from the initial relief at not finding her sister's dead body lying on the floor. "Are you calling me a liar? And what were you trying to do, screaming like that – frighten us to death? I thought you were being murdered! I can't believe you just fell out of bed!"

Emily carried on crying. "I want Mum, can't you go

and fetch her for me? I can't go on any more . . . honestly, I thought I was dying . . . and I thought you'd gone and left me here . . ." She held her chest in pain as she coughed again.

Maria strode over to her bag and pulled out a bottle of water. "Oh shut up and drink this," she said crossly, knowing that she was being unreasonable, but unable to stop herself. "Of course we wouldn't leave you here – we just went to look round. And for goodness sake stop going on about dying, it's only a cough! And tomorrow," she added, trying to get a grip on her emotions and sound more cheerful, "as long as you pull yourself together, we'll get to the cottage."

Maria lay awake for what seemed like hours that night, trying not to listen to Emily cough, desperately hoping that her sister would be well enough to cycle in the morning. Rufus had insisted on staying with Emily, which upset Maria, and to make matters worse her bed was too short and the musty smell of the drapes was suffocating. For what seemed like for ever Maria turned over and over on the ancient bed, heaving the throw over with her, her mind working overtime until she felt like screaming, she was so desperate to sleep.

When she finally dropped off she had an awful dream. Emily was dying. She was screaming for help, but Maria couldn't get to her because the ground was slipping from under her feet and some unseen, dark force was pulling Emily further and further away. When Maria woke in a cold sweat, what seemed like a million birds were singing the dawn chorus. She groaned, pulled the throw over her head and tried to go back to sleep.

With her ears covered, it was a little while before Maria realised that Emily was calling out, but as the calls got louder and louder, she pulled the rug from over her head and listened. Emily was obviously having a bad dream. Well, she's not the only one, thought Maria testily and tried to settle back down, but after a while she could ignore it no longer. "Oh, shut up," she muttered angrily under her breath. She threw off her throw and, hardly able to open her heavy eyelids, she staggered in to Emily's room, intending to give her a piece of her mind.

But when she saw her sister, her anger turned to fear. Emily had thrown off her blanket and was thrashing about on the bed, muttering and groaning. Her cheeks were burning feverishly red. Rufus was sitting next to her, licking her face. He whined when he saw Maria and looked up at her with worried eyes. Alarmed, Maria put a hand on her sister's forehead; it was burning hot, though the room was chilly from the damp morning air. "It's OK, Rufus," Maria murmured, more to herself than to the dog, but she knew it wasn't. In a panic, she tried to shake her sister awake. "Emily, Emily, it's me, Maria. For goodness sake wake up!" But when Emily sat up she looked at her out of unseeing eyes.

"Oh Mum, at last you've come," she murmured and lay back down again, gibbering something about sunbeds.

"No, Stupid, it's me, Maria," said Maria again, badly frightened. "You need a drink!" Then came a sound that chilled her to the core. The sound of a car engine. Rufus started to growl, then to bark.

"Hush, Rufus, good dog!" she urged him and ran to the window. A long, black limousine with darkened windows was approaching the gatehouse from the drive. It had begun to rain and the car's silvery headlights were piercing through the half-light of the wet morning. For a moment Maria stood rooted to the spot, watching the car, listening to the pitter-patter of raindrops on the window. "What are we going to do now, Rufus?" she whispered. He ran in to Arthur and barked. Maria followed him and shook Arthur.

"Arthur," she yelled desperately. "Emily's gone all weird and there's people coming! In a car! What are we going to do?"

"People coming here?" asked Arthur in surprise, rubbing his eyes and looking at his watch. "Now?"

Maria nodded desperately. "Hurry up!"

"That might be good," said Arthur, yawning, stretching and folding up his rug as coolly as if he were just off on a day trip. "They might help us." He walked up to the window and whistled. "Hey, just look at that car!"

"Never mind the stupid car, Emily's not well, get a move on!" yelled Maria, hardly able to contain her panic.

By the time Arthur reached Emily's room, the car had stopped outside the house. "A chauffeur's getting out!" whispered Maria frantically, watching out of a corner of the rain-spattered window. "In uniform. He's opening the door for . . . for a man. Just one man, wearing a suit." The click of the car doors closing sounded ominous somehow in the quiet of the early morning. The man in the suit stopped to examine the tyre marks on the lawns, made some sort of angry gesture, then ran up the flight of steps to the front door.

"They're coming in!" Maria continued in a panic-stricken whisper. "We'll have to hide!" Arthur nodded. He had been gathering their possessions together. Gently waking Emily, he draped her arm round his shoulders so that she was half walking, half carried.

"Where are we going?" mumbled Emily.

"Grab the bags!" Arthur ordered Maria. "What do you reckon on hiding in the stables? Then we'll listen out. If the man sounds friendly we'll make our presence known – he could be Minister for Culture or something, checking up. He might even give us a lift in his limousine!" Rufus growled again.

"Shhh, Rufus," said Maria in fear. Then she remembered something. "Our bikes! They'll find our bikes!"

"Too late to do anything about that," shrugged Arthur. "Don't forget Emily's blanket."

By the time they reached the kitchens, Maria could hear the man and his chauffeur coming towards them, looking in all the rooms, one by one. She was so scared, she could feel the hairs on her arms and neck prickling. One of the men, presumably the boss, was doing a lot of shouting; mostly swear words. Catching snatches of what he was saying, Maria gathered that he had expected the furniture to still be there and by the language he was using, he was obviously furious that it had gone. She knew the words; some of them she used herself, but coming from this man they took on a whole new meaning, ugly and vicious. He certainly didn't sound like a culture minister. He sounded rough and cruel.

"Forget the lift," Arthur whispered to Maria.

Maria didn't bother to reply, she was too busy trying to manage all the bags and not trip over Emily's throw that she hadn't had time to fold. Rufus trotted at her heels. "Keep quiet, Rufus, quiet," Maria kept urging him and he blinked at her silently as if he understood. The back door, though heavy, opened easily. Arthur helped Emily down on to the wet flagstones beneath the nearest window and indicated to Maria to join them. Dropping the bags and rugs next to Emily, Maria pulled the back door closed as quietly as she could, then joined her companions. Arthur hugged Rufus close to the wall, whispering to him to be quiet and stroking him reassuringly. Maria was scared stiff. Her heart seemed to thump louder and louder as she heard the men's voices and footsteps getting nearer and nearer. Rufus' ears pricked and she glared at him warningly, terrified that he would give them away.

"Why . . ." began Emily groggily, but Maria quickly clapped a hand over her mouth.

"When I find out who's done this . . ." yelled a threatening voice from just the other side of the wall. Arthur grimaced. Maria was terrified. Rain dripped down her face, but she didn't dare move her hand to wipe the drops away. She closed her eyes. The man must be looking out of the very window under which they were hiding. Surely he must be able to hear her heart beating.

The cool morning air and the rain seemed to be reviving Emily. She pushed Maria's hand away and whispered, "What are we doing here?" Maria desperately motioned to her to be quiet. She didn't have time to feel relieved that Emily was sounding better. At any moment she expected the back door to burst open and their hiding place to be discovered.

"Just wait till I get my hands on those thieves!" yelled the man menacingly, then he seemed to turn and his voice faded in to the distance. After a while, Arthur cautiously peered over the windowsill.

"We've got to go and hide in the stables over there," Maria mouthed to Emily, who nodded silently in reply, wide-eyed and scared.

"Now!" whispered Arthur urgently and they ran low, Arthur helping Emily along. Maria had so much to carry that she had to let go of Rufus' collar and to her horror he barked, twice, loudly, before they all bundled through the half-open stable door. Blinking in the unaccustomed darkness, Arthur whispered urgently, "Here!" and they all scrambled behind a stack of hay bales next to the tack room.

Just at that moment the back door of the house burst open. "I tell you I heard a dog!" the rough man shouted menacingly. "When I catch it I'll shoot it!" Then he let off a gun, twice. The shots echoed round the countryside and the three fugitives stared at each other in silent horror. Emily stifled a cough and Maria pulled Rufus closer, her heart pounding with terror. He whined and leaned his head against her knee.

Only the patter of the raindrops on the dirty window broke the sickening silence. Then they heard the man say something else and go running back into the house.

"Bikes," was the only word Maria heard, but it wasn't said in a very pleasant way. A ray of hopeful sunshine shone through the window to lighten the darkness for a few seconds, but was quickly extinguished by ominously gathering black clouds, like a pack of hungry, slavering wolves, moving in for the kill. Maria shuddered, not so much with the damp and cold, but with fear.

twenty-five

"What now?" whispered Maria fiercely to Arthur, as if everything was his fault. "What about your God looking after us now then? They know we're here. They're going to shoot Rufus and they've got our bikes! They'll probably kill us all!"

"They won't kill us!" answered Arthur gently, pulling two more bales of hay round them, to fence them in. In doing so he uncovered a leaflet advertising the house and gardens. He picked it up and wiped it on his sleeve. "We'll get out of here somehow. Look! There's a map of this place here – maybe there's a way out through the woods behind us."

"We'll have to make a run for it," said Maria, swallowing hard. "They must think it's us who nicked their stuff. You feeling better, Em? Think you could run?"

"I'm not sure," replied Emily weakly. She coughed, then closed her eyes and settled herself into the loose hay behind her. "I'll try." Maria watched her anxiously for a minute. It didn't look promising. Emily hadn't even asked who the man was or why they were hiding. Still, at least she wasn't moaning or hallucinating any more.

Grabbing the leaflet out of Arthur's hands, Maria

studied the map, Arthur leaning over her shoulder. They pored over it, hoping that an entrance might appear, preferably behind them, but it was no good. There was no back entrance or even side entrance; the only way in and out was through the main gates. Maria felt desperate.

"We don't have to go down the drive, we could go round the edge of the horse's field," Arthur suggested.

"But if they see us they'll shoot Rufus," wailed Maria desperately. "And how are we going to get Emily to run?" She looked over at Emily and her heart sank. She seemed to have gone back to sleep. "Look at the state of her! We've got to get our bikes back," she said, knowing that she was suggesting the impossible. Even if they did have their bikes, Emily couldn't cycle any more than she could run.

"I've got an idea," Arthur whispered. "I'll cause a diversion."

"What do you mean?"

"I'll run round, the opposite way to the drive, then while the men are chasing me, you and Emily get away from here as fast as you can."

"Don't be pathetic, Arthur, they've got a gun – they'll shoot you!"

"They'll never get me!" said Arthur light-heartedly.

"No, Arthur, don't be stupid, you'll get yourself killed," argued Maria. "Anyway, they might split up. For goodness sake, think of something else."

It was quiet in the stables, quiet and dark and it smelled pleasantly of horses, hay and polished leather. The only sound was the rain pattering gently on the roof.

Closing her eyes, Maria could pretend to be in the local stables at home, but the pounding in her heart gave her away and when she opened her eyes, everything was still the same. "Arthur, what are we going to do?" she wailed. "We've got to get out of here! Now!"

Arthur looked up from the leaflet. "Wow, you're not going to believe this!" he exclaimed with an awed whisper. "That bed you slept in last night, Queen Elizabeth the First slept there! Can you believe it?" Maria glared at him in disbelief.

"Arthur, for goodness sake, we're just about to die and all you can . . ." she hissed fiercely. Suddenly she stopped and stiffened in fear as she heard the back door of the house open. Footsteps began to click-click slowly across the flagstones of the courtyard. The person paused, as Arthur and Maria had done last night, to look in the windows of the restaurant and gift shop, before coming towards the stables. "They're looking for us!" Maria whispered, eyes wide in fear. She sank further down behind the hay bales. Arthur put his finger to his lips.

The time it took for the footsteps to reach the stables seemed like an eternity. Maria hardly dared to breathe. Thank goodness Emily was asleep. Rufus was listening to the footsteps, his hackles rising, ready to spring. Maria hugged him tight. "No, Rufus," she whispered to him sternly, as he sat up, alert and ready to spring. She stroked his head gently. "No barkies." Tears sprang to her eyes and she gritted her teeth. That mean old man would have to kill her before he shot her dog!

A stream of murky daylight entered the stables as the

old door opened wider. The rain, which was getting heavier, suddenly sounded louder. The man stepped in a few paces and paused. Maria swallowed hard. She couldn't see him, but she imagined him looking round. Did the hay bales look as if they had just been moved? She held her breath, silently begging Rufus not to bark, as she listened to the menacing footsteps reach the display of farm machinery at the other end of the building, then walk slowly back to the door. Go away, just go away, Maria begged silently, but it seemed that the man was reluctant to leave the shelter of the barn. She heard him light a cigarette before a curl of acrid tobacco smoke wafted towards their hiding place.

"He hasn't seen us," mouthed Arthur. "As soon as the coast's clear we'll run for the field, OK? Leave the bags . . ."

Maria was just about to reply when Emily coughed. Maria and Arthur stared helplessly at each other as they heard the footsteps turn. "No!" whispered Maria, clutching Rufus and closing her eyes.

When she opened them again, Maria realised that she was looking at the astonished face of the liveried chauffeur. "Well I'm blowed! A bunch o' kids!" said the chauffeur. "This ain't a good place for you to be right now!" Maria stared up at him and Rufus growled. Maria put a warning hand on his collar. She had lost the power of speech, but the man's startled face looked kindly enough. And he wasn't carrying a gun.

An impatient shout from the back door of the house made her gulp hard. "Cooper?" yelled the man. "Where the hell are you?" The chauffeur hurried back out into the courtyard. "Found anything yet?" shouted the man, when he saw his chauffeur appear.

Maria was breathing hard. "No sign of life round here, Mr Oliver, sir," called back the chauffeur. She and Arthur exchanged an astonished glance. "Of course, sir," Maria heard him say in a deferential tone, as the chauffeur reached the back door, "it might be someone different who committed the theft. After all, sir, on *bikes* . . ."

"You're too soft, Cooper," they heard Mr Oliver snarl. "Anyone entering my house without my permission deserves death, same as the thieves of my property. There's a new law round here now. Mine. And I don't take prisoners. Thank God Anderson and his team will be here later – protect this place properly. God help any trespassers then!" He laughed, cruelly.

"Very good, sir," came the voice of the chauffeur. "Did you want me to keep looking for the owners of the bikes, sir?"

"No." Mr Oliver dropped his voice slightly and Maria had to strain to hear through the open door. "Get the car ready, I've just heard from Nolan. He's making a drop at the Three Horseshoes. We'll sort the rest out later – with reinforcements."

Maria still hadn't seen Mr Oliver close up, but she didn't need to, she could tell what sort of man he was from the tone of his voice. Evil. She vaguely wondered what he meant about there being a new law now and someone making a drop, but she didn't have time to consider for long. She heard him stride away, but Mr

Cooper's footsteps were coming back. Maria gulped. Would the chauffeur want something in return for his silence? Emily began to snore gently and Rufus started growling again. "Hush, Rufus," Maria urged him.

"You want to get out of here fast," said the chauffeur on his return. "Mr Oliver's in a right temper since someone's stolen his precious antiques. It weren't anything to do with you I suppose?" They shook their heads. "Didn't think so. What's the matter with the young 'un?" he added, nodding towards Emily, who was moaning in her sleep.

"She's got a cough," replied Maria, finding her tongue at last. "Thanks for not telling," she added and Arthur nodded his thanks too.

"Listen," said the man. "The Boss ain't as bad as he sounds, but he's taking over this part of the country – it's every man for himself now, so he's got to be tough. I'm afraid he's ruined your bikes, so when you hear us go, you leg it, right? You need to get your little friend there to safety. We'll be away about an hour I should think, but don't hang about. This place'll look like Fort Knox by tonight."

"Cooper!" yelled the boss.

"Good luck!" whispered the chauffeur, beating a hasty retreat. "And don't forget, get out of here fast!"

"How are we supposed to get out of here fast without our bikes?" muttered Maria darkly.

Arthur smiled. "It was good of him not to let on."

Maria rolled her eyes and tried not to let the tears escape. "Arthur, what are you smiling about, don't you understand?" she wailed. "We'll have to walk – run! For miles and miles! Right now!" She looked towards her sister. "How are we supposed to get Emily to do that?"

twenty-six

To Maria's annoyance, Arthur continued absent-mindedly to peruse his leaflet, then suddenly he peered round the hay to the other end of the building and grinned. Maria grimaced. Being cheerful was one thing, but in their present circumstances it was simply infuriating. She looked the other way, but Arthur waved the leaflet in front of her until she grabbed it angrily out of his hand. However, catching sight of a photograph of the horse from last night, Maria was suddenly interested. The mare was pulling a little farm cart, which had been converted to take visitors for rides around the grounds.

"There's our answer!" grinned Arthur, as Maria looked up. "Emily can sleep in the back!" Maria peered round the hay as Arthur had done. There was the old cart, just waiting to be used . . . But they didn't know how to hitch the horse to the cart, let alone drive it. She looked at Arthur's expectant face. He thought she could do it. Maria swallowed. She looked in turn at the picture on the leaflet, the cart, then at Emily's sleeping form. She would have to try. She had seen it done; it couldn't be that difficult – and imagine everyone's faces when she arrived at the cottage driving a horse and cart!

"Arthur, you're so annoying!" she whispered, but her smile betrayed her true feelings.

Arthur crept to the door. Through a crack in the wood he watched the limousine swish away down the wet drive. "They've gone!" he called, running down to the cart. "They turned right, so when we go, we'd better go left."

"That's OK, we won't want to go back to the main road – too much traffic for a horse and cart." Maria lay a rug over her sleeping sister, then followed Arthur to the other end of the building. Close up, the cart looked bigger than it did in the picture; it would be an awful responsibility to drive, even on the country roads. She swallowed. Arthur was looking over a diagram he had taken off the wall of how to hitch the horse to the cart. "You can do it, can't you?" he asked.

Maria snatched the laminated sheet out of Arthur's hand, scanned quickly over the information and peered through the tack room window. "Sure," she answered loftily, feeling deeply grateful to the artist for the neat drawing. It had to work. It just had to. They could be home in no time with a cart! She swallowed. "They're all a bit different of course. It might take a while . . . we'll get the cart out before I fetch the horse. We'd better hurry."

"No problemo!" grinned Arthur, looking relieved. "Operation Escape! Yes, sir! I mean, Ma'am!" He swung open the big double doors at the other end of the building without difficulty, but the cart refused to budge.

"Are you pushing, Arthur?" called Maria irritably from the front of the cart.

"As hard as I can!" replied Arthur cheerfully. "Do we

have a hitch? Hitch, horse, cart, get it?" Maria hardly heard him.

"Why won't it move?" she muttered, then she twigged. "It's got a brake!" Arthur laughed, but Maria was furious with herself. She hadn't thought about the brake. What else might she not think about?

Even with the brake off, pushing the cart out to the wet courtyard was hard work. Maria checked her watch, wiped the sweat from her forehead and pursed her lips. Maybe taking the cart was a mistake. But that awful man would be back in fifty minutes, maybe less; there was no choice. Her heart beat faster as she ran back into the building. She would just have to do the best she could.

"What next?" called Arthur.

"Harness!" The tack room was locked, but with one huge shove of Maria's shoulder to the dry, old wood, the door burst open. She gave Arthur the collar to carry.

"What is this thing for?" asked Arthur incredulously, staggering as he lifted it. "It's a tonne weight!"

"It's part of the harness. Goes round the horse's neck. Just dump it down by the cart."

"Round its neck? You're joking! What is it, a noose or something? And if I put it down it'll get wet."

"For goodness sake stop going on Arthur, I need to think!" begged Maria, gathering up the various pieces of the bridle.

Arthur nodded and stood to attention. "Yes, Ma'am! I await your further orders!" She ignored him. Her head was spinning. Cart. Harness. Fetch the horse. Maria grabbed a head collar, a lead rope and a couple of apples.

Dashing back outside, she was furious to find Arthur throwing a stick for Rufus. "Rufus loves this!" called Arthur, laughing. "He doesn't mind the rain. Look at him go!" Rufus certainly seemed to be enjoying himself. He barked and jumped up at the stick, then tore away across the grass to fetch it.

Maria gritted her teeth and stamped her foot. "What do you think this is?" she yelled. "A holiday camp? Can't you do something useful, like get our stuff in the cart? And check on Emily. I'm going to get the horse."

"Sorry," said Arthur and ran back to the stable, looking sheepish. Rufus chased after him with the stick in his mouth.

"And keep Rufus with you," Maria shouted back as she started running for the field, "in case the horse isn't used to dogs. And get as much feed from the feed bins as you can in the cart. And straw and hay if there's room."

After a few paces Maria stopped running. She didn't want the horse to pick up on her fear. And there was no doubt about it, she was afraid. Her heart was pounding, she was shaking and her breath was coming in gasps. She closed her eyes, took a few deep breaths and counted slowly to ten. "It's just Saturday morning and we're going for a ride," she told herself nonchalantly, then repeated it twice, out loud, until it sounded almost believable. Well it was Saturday morning, anyway. She wiped the rain from her face, pulled up the collar of her jacket to stop the drips from going down her neck and forced herself to walk at a leisurely pace up to the gate.

The horse came straight to Maria, or rather, straight to

the apple she was holding out in her hand. In spite of herself, Maria couldn't help smiling. Talk about cupboard love!

The poor horse looked even more bedraggled now than she had last night, or maybe it was just more noticeable in daylight. Her tail was a matted mess and big muddy drips were oozing down her mane. She looked as though she had just been rolling on the wet grass; patches of mud were plastered over her flanks and she was losing her winter coat, which didn't help. Maria patted her and a handful of dirty wet hair came away in her hand. If I get found with this horse I could be done for neglect, thought Maria grimly, wiping her hand on her jeans. Why, oh why did it have to rain again today?

It wasn't easy trying to balance reassuring the horse with hurrying. Maria's heart was beating fit to bust in her chest, but while the horse was munching, she slipped the head collar over the mare's head. She didn't seem to be at all perturbed to see Maria instead of her previous owner. Thanks to the apples, thought Maria wryly.

Arthur waved cheerily as Maria returned to the courtyard with the horse, who seemed a slow and steady sort; eager to be out, but not jumpy and fortunately not upset by Rufus' presence. "Emily's still coughing, but she's asleep," called Arthur. "And I've sorted out our things in the cart."

Maria put on a know-all expression. "Thanks. Here's our horse. Hold her for a minute for me, would you, while I sort out the harness?"

Arthur was pleased. "Sure." He stroked the horse's

nose and she nuzzled him gently. He took a step back and laughed. "Are all horses as friendly as this one?"

"Some. Pass me the bridle."

"What's that?"

"That thing there with the reins, that's it."

Slipping the head collar down round her neck, Maria offered the bit to the horse. She obligingly took it in her mouth and Maria pulled the bridle up and over her ears, while Arthur looked on in open-mouthed admiration.

"Wow, Maria, you're amazing!" he grinned.

"It's easy when you know how," Maria answered loftily, making a start on the buckles, but inside she was just grateful that the horse was willing.

Arthur patted her. "Has she got a name?"

"I don't know."

"We can't just keep calling her 'horse' – how about we give her a name?"

"If you like."

"How about Buttercup?"

"Arthur, for goodness sake, that's a cow's name!"

"It doesn't have to be!"

"Look, she's not going to be Buttercup, OK?"

"OK. What about Daisy?"

"Arthur!"

"What?"

"Don't you know anything? Daisy's a cow's name too!"

"No way! One of my mates has got a little sister called Daisy."

"Can't you think of an African name for her?"

"We don't have horses where I come from. We have

mangoes, though. We could call her Mango!"

Maria paused to look at Arthur. She couldn't make out if he was winding her up or not; he was grinning, but that was nothing unusual. She decided not to take the bait. "I know, we'll call her Parly, short for Parlingworth," she decided, "because she comes from Parlingworth House."

Arthur laughed. "I still prefer Mango!"

Maria didn't care what he preferred. She was trying not to frown as she stared at the diagram from the stable that was coming in far more useful than the creator of the museum could possibly have anticipated. Putting the bridle on the horse was relatively simple; adding the collar and cart was something else. Parly backed up to the cart obligingly when Maria gave her a shove from the front, to more admiring glances from Arthur, but after that things became more complicated. There were so many loops and buckles, the collar was so heavy and Maria was in such a state of panic that it all got a bit confusing. The atmosphere grew more and more tense as straps became twisted, Maria got cross, the rain eased off then got worse again and time marched irrepressibly on. Even Arthur started to frown when he looked at his watch. Only Parly remained calm and stood quietly crunching the bit in her mouth, while Rufus ran about in the wood behind them, chasing rabbits.

But at last the harness was on. Despite the rain and the morning chill, Maria was sweating as she swiftly checked over her handiwork, comparing it to the diagram in her hand. It had to be right.

"Maria, you're brilliant!" said Arthur, patting Parly and

looking at the horse and cart in admiration.

"I know," she replied loftily, but deep inside her stomach was churning. She wiped the wet hair out of her eyes. Suppose something wasn't right or Parly didn't respond to her commands? It had dawned on her, too, that just getting out of the grounds in an hour might not be enough to ensure their safety; they might be followed. After all, they were taking the horse and cart. Stealing, sort of. Mr Oliver didn't seem to be too keen on that, and he had a gun. Maria wondered if Arthur would consider this to be stealing, too, but she didn't mention it; she could do without him backing out on her now. "How much longer?" she asked.

"Eight minutes," replied Arthur soberly, wiping the rain from his watch. Maria was stunned. Eight minutes!

"That's it then!" she yelled. "Get Emily! We need to get out of here!"

twenty-seven

Maria suddenly felt a pang of guilt. She hadn't thought about Emily for a while. As she quickly worked around Parly's hooves with a pick, she tried to convince herself that it was Emily's fault; if she hadn't got a stupid cough, she could have done some of the work instead of just lying there. But her conscience didn't quite buy it.

Rufus jumped obligingly up into the cart when Maria called him and he sat on a bench as if he travelled in a cart every day of his life. "I love you, Rufus," crooned Maria, reaching up to pat him. "Don't worry, we'll be safe soon. I'll never let that man get you."

Arthur had made a good job of packing the cart, Maria noticed approvingly; everything was stored neatly and he had taken a good supply of feed, a sack each of carrots and pony nuts and a bag of apples. He had packed hay and blankets under one of the benches, two bales of straw under another and in a corner was an assortment of brushes for Parly and various other old farm implements, along with a length of rope and another laminated sheet about caring for horses. So Arthur did have some brains!

Maria climbed up to the driving seat, reins in hand and with a resigned grimace, wiped the wet wood with her sleeve. "I'll groom you as soon as I can, darling," she assured the muddy horse, looking round anxiously for Arthur and Emily. The eight minutes were running out. What was keeping them?

Maria stared in horror when Arthur returned. He was carrying Emily, who had her eyes closed. "She doesn't look too good," said Arthur, looking worried. "I can't wake her up. I've prayed for her, but we need to get her to your dad. He's a doctor, isn't he?" Maria nodded and swallowed. Arthur settled Emily in the recovery position on a collection of rugs in the bottom of the cart between the seats. She didn't move and her chest rattled with every breath. Arthur looked up at Maria. He wasn't smiling. "Better go," he suggested.

Maria turned round, took a deep breath and released the brake, blinking away the tears that had sprung uninvited to her eyes. Maybe this was the end, she thought desperately. Everything seemed to be against them. Why bother to fight any longer? Maybe the people who died in London were the lucky ones – at least they had gone quickly. Maria's mind flashed back to the pall of smoke that she had seen rising; she tried to shake it away, but the darkness seemed to spread out, as if trying to reach her too.

"Walk on," she urged Parly and with a flick of the reins, the horse set off, head held high. A split second later the cart jolted forwards. Maria and Arthur were jerked backwards by the sudden movement and Emily slid across the floor of the cart, landing with a bump against the sacks of feed.

"What's happening?" she asked weakly, opening her eyes and trying to sit up.

"Emily's woken up!" Arthur shouted to Maria over the noise of the cart and the horse's hooves on the harsh stone. Maria didn't dare to turn round, but she had heard her sister.

"Hi Emily!" she called back. The relief was indescribable. The cart was moving safely, too. Nothing had fallen off yet! Maria shook away despair and gritted her teeth in determination as they successfully crossed the courtyard and joined the main drive. They would make it to the cottage! They would, they would, somehow they would.

The mare obeyed willingly as Maria turned her through the gatehouse and down the drive towards the main gates. As soon as the going was smoother, Maria urged Parly to a trot and she obliged. The cart jolted up and down so badly that Maria bit her tongue, but it was wonderful to have the house behind them and the speed was exhilarating. Congratulating herself on doing an excellent job, Maria took a more confident grip on the reins and laughed out loud as the cool air whooshed past her face. Yes! They were out of here! As if in confirmation of Maria's new hope, the sun broke through the clouds in a blaze of glorious light, making the world sparkle and dance through the raindrops as the cart sped along the path to freedom. She grinned. At least the sun was on their side!

"It's well bumpy, it's making Rufus jump up and down!" Arthur called to Maria. "It's so funny, I wish you could see him!" But Maria was concentrating on her driving and her eyes were fixed on the way ahead. She had noticed something odd. The gates weren't open as they had been last night. Worse, as they drew near, Maria could make out a large padlocked chain wrapped around the metal bars, twinkling in the sun. She stared in disbelief and called Parly to a halt, pulling back on the reins and throwing the brake. The sudden stillness was electrifying. No, Maria whispered silently to herself, wildly searching with her eyes for a gap in the long row of trees, to no avail. This couldn't be happening, not now they had come this far! The cheerful sun was just a trick . . .

Maria turned round in surprise as Arthur jumped out of the cart. She could hardly believe her eyes as she watched him run to the gates and clip the chains with one of the farm implements that he had collected. As soon as he had finished the job Arthur swung open the gates and leaped back in the cart.

"OK, let's go!" he called. "To Dover and beyond!"

"How did you know it was padlocked?" Maria yelled back as she clicked to Parly.

"Divine inspiration!" he replied cheerfully. Whatever, thought Maria. At least they were out of here!

Parly tossed her head as if in surprise at leaving the drive, but obeyed without the slightest hesitation. "How many minutes now?" called back Maria, urging Parly to a trot along the empty country lane. She hardly dared to believe that they had escaped! There was a pause.

"Minus five." Maria caught her breath. Nobody said anything.

Driving along the country lane, Maria's head began to

pound and the sick feeling returned. How long would it take for Mr Oliver to find the gates open and realise that the horse and cart had gone? Scanning the road ahead anxiously for a turning, she hoped desperately that one would appear before the limousine. A cloud passed over the sun and a chill, damp breeze made Maria shiver.

A muddy field on the left seemed to pass very slowly, but as they rounded a bend, Arthur gave a yell. "Crossroads ahead!" he shouted. Maria's heart leaped. She urged Parly to go a little faster, which she seemed to do with relish, but before they reached the junction, she heard the sound of an engine approaching from behind.

Maria's heart was in her mouth. "Please God, no,' she begged silently as the engine got closer, but it was only a little red Fiat. "Steady girl, steady," Maria reassured the horse as the car slowed down to overtake. A little girl waved out of the rear window, but Maria didn't have time to wave back; she clung to the reins, holding a nervous Parly on course, hoping that all the drivers they met would be as courteous.

There was no signpost, but Maria followed her instincts and turned right at the crossroads, then quite soon, without stopping, took a left turn just before a village. The lanes were narrow and winding and the constant jolting was wearing, but Maria was hesitant to slow down.

"Do you know where you're going?" called Arthur, a little while and several turnings later.

"No," Maria shouted back. "Just as far away from that horrible man as possible. He's a crook. That house doesn't belong to him any more than it belongs to us.

He's got a nerve, threatening us like that. Do you reckon we're safe yet?"

"If I had a limousine, I wouldn't bring it down here, would you?"

"What?" It was difficult to hear above the horse's hooves and the racing wheels.

"I said, if I had a limousine, I wouldn't bring it down here." Maria thought about it. The road they were now on was hardly more than a farm track. Arthur had a point. She turned round and smiled.

"We're safe then?"

"I suppose so!"

It was a glorious feeling, despite being damp, tired, stiff, hungry and thirsty. Maria slowed Parly to a walk, gave her lots of praise for being such a wonderful saviour and yawned and stretched with relief. The warmth from the sun on Maria's face seemed to reach right inside her. Surely they would be home soon – and now, as well as a dog, she had a horse! Maria chuckled to herself as she imagined her dad's face when she turned up with her new pets. Arthur seemed cheerful, too. He passed Maria a can of lemonade and a slightly squashed apricot pie with a big grin. "Last edibles," he told her, "so make the most of them!"

Maria demolished the pie and gulped the lemonade. It was a long overdue breakfast. "How's Emily?" she asked as she ate.

"Gone back to sleep. Really deeply. I tried to give her a drink, but she didn't wake up. The sooner we get her to your dad the better."

"Yeah." Maria suddenly realised that it was too soon to

be congratulating herself on their escape; they weren't home yet. And all of a sudden, she remembered her mother's handbag and the pool of blood. Getting to the cottage had always been their aim, but now that their goal was nearer, she began to wonder about it. So far she had managed to blot out such thoughts, but suppose they reached the cottage and found it empty, looted and abandoned, or discovered the mutilated remains of corpses there? Dread began to well up inside Maria's tired mind. "No!" she suddenly said to herself boldly, sitting up straight. "It's not going to be like that!" Instead, she forced herself to imagine everyone (alive and well, of course) coming out to greet them, having heard the sound of horse's hooves on the drive. They would be surprised and pleased to see them, and full of admiration for Maria, then they would take Emily in and Dad would make her better, while Mum would fuss round, sorting out beds and flowers. Grandpa would help with Parly, cracking jokes, while Granny would make a hot meal and a cup of tea . . . Then Maria imagined herself sinking into a luxuriously steaming bath, full of fragrant bubbles – that was such a wonderful thought! She would stay there for at least an hour, topping up the hot water every now and then . . . It was a pleasant little scene. But the pie and lemonade sat heavily in Maria's stomach. She sighed and looked round at the sky. At least there hadn't been any more planes. Not yet, anyway.

They passed more fields, more trees, a silent railway line and seemingly unending hedgerows as the cart rattled, creaked and bumped on and on. It was like being trapped in an ancient computer game with boring graphics. There didn't seem to be any signposts and it was impossible to ascertain how far they might have come. They surely must be getting near the coast now though, Maria reasoned, scrutinising the view for any clues as to their whereabouts without success. Funny that there weren't any signposts, even at junctions.

Something else was bothering Maria more than their direction. Something she had put off asking, ever since they had set off from the garden centre, but at last she plucked up the courage. "Do you want me to drop you off in Dover?" she asked Arthur nonchalantly. He didn't hesitate with his answer.

"No, I'll see you home first."

"OK." Despite his offer sounding terribly old-fashioned, it was exactly what Maria wanted to hear. Never mind being feminist and independent, she didn't like the idea of doing any part of the journey alone, however short. And if something awful had happened at the cottage, at least Arthur would help her to decide what to do. "Mum or my grandpa can drive you to the port. Unless you want to stay for a while," she assured him.

"Thanks for the offer, but I need to get to my family."

"'Course." Maria tried to sound cheerful. There was a pause. "I hope you find them OK."

"I will, don't worry. I'll miss you two though," he admitted. Rufus barked at a rabbit running along the grassy bank. "Sorry, you three!"

"Four," Maria corrected him. "Don't forget Parly!"

Arthur laughed. "I will never in my life forget dear

Mango! I've written a little ode to her, do you want to hear it?"

"You've written a little what?" asked Maria incredulously, turning round to see if she could tell from Arthur's face if he was mocking her or not.

He was grinning in his usual cheerful way. "An ode. You know, a poem."

Maria turned back round. "You've written an ode to Parly? What on? What for?"

"In my head, to give me something to think about."

"Arthur, you're crazy."

"Well, do you want to hear it or not?"

Maria shrugged. "If you like."

Arthur began in a dramatic voice, as if he were reciting Shakespeare.

Dear Mango, you have saved my life
When I thought all was lost
My bicycle was just a wreck,
But you counted not the cost
And helped me just when things seemed grim
With men with guns behind
You took us safely home to bed
Dear Parly, you are kind!

Maria turned and grimaced at him. "That is such a load of rubbish, Arthur. Did you really just make that up?"

"Of course I did!"

"Just now?"

"Yes, I just said so!"

"Well, don't give up the day job!"

Arthur hooted with laughter and Maria realised with a jolt that she was going to miss Arthur when he left. He wasn't just useful, he was maybe the best friend she had ever had and today he was going to leave her, who knows how long for – maybe for ever. As she blinked back sudden tears, Maria realised that her emotions were fraying at the edges. She had had enough. Enough of loss, fear and the uncertain future. Enough of making difficult decisions, enough of Emily being ill and enough of this awful journey. Despite her best effort, she couldn't stop the tears falling, so she allowed them to drip silently down her cheeks and on to her jacket, for no particular reason, or maybe for everything, until they ran dry.

After a while Maria called back to Arthur, "Parly must be getting thirsty. Could you look out for a stream or something?"

"Sure," replied Arthur. "Does she drink water then?"

Maria was staggered at the stupidity of the question. "Water? Nah, our Parly, she's got class. She likes vodka and Martini, shaken not stirred," she replied. There was a moment's silence, then Arthur let out such a loud hoot of laughter that Maria jumped. She pretended not to have heard.

"Vodka and . . . ha, ha, ha . . . vodka and . . . vod . . . vodka and Martini!" exploded Arthur. "Ha, ha! A horse! On a bar stool . . . ha, ha, ha!"

Maria turned round to give him a withering look, but she couldn't help smiling at his helpless laughter. "It wasn't that funny!"

"Sipping it through a . . . ha, ha, ha, a sss, ha, ha, ha, through a ssstraw! Ha, ha, ha, ha ha!"

Tears began to run down Arthur's cheeks and he was holding his sides. "On the rocks!" he spat out, hardly able to control himself.

Maria shrugged nonchalantly and turned round, but she allowed herself to grin when he couldn't see and her hopes lifted as she listened to Arthur's laughter and saw in the distance a group of houses.

"Well, this will be something to tell the grandchildren," Arthur called to Maria, once he had recovered his equilibrium.

Maria was so taken aback she could barely speak. "*Grandchildren*?" she spluttered. "Arthur you're crazy! And I never ever want to remember this. Ever. If we get home, I'm going to delete all this. Forget it. For ever. Wash it away in the bath."

"Well, you certainly could do with a wash!"

Maria turned and glowered evilly at him, but couldn't help grinning at his ridiculous face, as he shielded himself with his arm, pretending to be afraid of her.

As they plodded their way through the eerily silent hamlet, which seemed to have no name, it dawned on Maria that there had been no signs on any of the villages that they had passed. Maybe somebody had removed them deliberately, so people got lost. That was scary. And there was still no sign of Dover or the sea. No sight or sound. They ought at least to be able to hear traffic from the motorway, surely. What was this place? She pulled Parly to a halt on a slight incline next to an old pub with black paint scrawled over its name. The never-ending clip-clop of the horse's hooves and rolling of the cartwheels came to an abrupt halt. The quietness was almost tangible. Maria stood up gingerly. She could hear nothing but leaves rustling in the breeze and a circle of rooks cawing above the church spire of another village, not far away. Looking round in every direction, she could see nothing but trees, fields and the odd cluster of farm buildings. So where was Dover? Which way was the coast?

Arthur looked up at her enquiringly. Maria shrugged, sat down, clicked to Parly and the cart jerked once more in to action. She didn't want to admit it out loud, but an awful thought had filled Maria with dread. Maybe, all the time they had thought that they were heading for the coast, they had just been going round in a big circle.

twenty-eight

Parly plodded steadily on, past interminable fields; fields of sheep and lambs, fields of nodding grasses, fields of plastic cloches and orchards of blooming fruit trees in rigid rows. Maria was becoming increasingly tired and sluggish. Home-please, home-please, Maria's mind repeated to itself to the rhythm of Parly's hooves, as her eyelids became heavier and heavier. It seemed as if they were stuck in a weird time warp. Where were they? Did it really matter any more? Was this all a trap? How much further did they have to go? The trees and hedgerows sat in obstinate silence, refusing to tell.

As they passed a short row of boarded-up cottages, a sudden trio of herring gulls calling noisily overhead made Maria jump and Rufus bark. "Seagulls!" called Arthur excitedly. "We must be near the sea!"

"They do go quite a few miles inland," replied Maria casually, but inside her heart began to beat faster as they passed a sign for a T-junction. Maybe . . .

At the junction, where their lane joined a slightly wider country road, they had a choice of left or right. A van zoomed along the road, which made Parly jump. She shot forward, tossing her head. Maria was nearly jerked off her seat, but was glad to see the van. Life at last! "Whoa!" she called to Parly and the cart bumped to a halt. Arthur jumped down and crossed the road to uncover a signpost from the growing hedgerow.

"Dover's back the way we came," he called, after a pause.

Maria was horrified. "It can't be!"

"That's what it says. And the sun's behind us, more or less, so we must be heading north; is that right?"

Maria turned round to look at the sun, hoping for inspiration, but none came. How did you use the sun as a compass? Should they be heading north? She frowned. This was ridiculous. How was she supposed to know? "It doesn't say Callum, does it?" Maria asked, referring to the signpost, hardly daring to hope. Dover couldn't be the other way, it just couldn't! She nearly screamed. This was the news she had dreaded. But Arthur shook his head.

"There's no Callum. Offingworth ring any bells?" It didn't.

"I suppose you can't turn the cart round?" asked Arthur hopefully.

"Don't be stupid."

"OK." They both looked round anxiously as Emily coughed and moaned in her sleep. "Take your pick then, left or right!"

"But they're both wrong!"

There was a pause. "Maybe there'll be another junction soon. Or some houses. Bound to be some sooner or later, or we'll see somebody – we'll stop and ask the way." Arthur climbed back into the cart and bent over Emily.

Maria's face was grim. Eeny, meeny, miney, right, she decided and clicked to Parly.

In the first five minutes, two cars passed them in the opposite direction, but neither of them was Mum's or Dad's. Of course they weren't. Nobody knew where they were now. They didn't even know themselves.

In a way, Maria was so desperate to get to the cottage that she felt she would burst. But at the same time, the deep dread of finding something awful held her back. Fear of the unknown, Maria muttered to herself and tried to daydream of a date with Adam Johanssen, but somehow the magic between them had gone. Even the memory of his face had faded and he seemed to belong to a strange, long distant past.

Before long, a large white delivery van drew up behind them. There wasn't enough room for it to pass on the road; the cart was taking up too much room. The driver revved his engine several times, then wound down his window. "Get out the way, Pikies, I haven't got all day!" he shouted.

"Just ignore him," Arthur advised, but Maria had seen a passing space a little way ahead, at the entrance to a field. "Come on, Parly, come on," Maria sang out as reassuringly as she could manage, urging the mare to a trot, but the noise of the revving engine was making Parly nervous and she began to jump and snort.

Maria desperately tried to pull the horse in towards the gate to the field, but they were only halfway there when the man in the van honked his horn and held it down. It spooked Parly. She started to side-step and shy and the cart swung even further out in to the road. Maria started to panic. "Just wait a minute, you road hog!" she shouted to the man, but he probably didn't hear her above the noise of his engine. He drew right up to the cart.

"Get off the road with that heap of junk!" he yelled, leaning out of his window. "You're a danger to the public!" He blasted his horn again, long and loud. Parly jumped again in fear. Maria clung on to the reins with all her might. The cart swung back in, but the man roared past them impatiently before there was enough room and his van knocked the back of the cart with a sharp crack as he passed.

"Idiot!" yelled Maria, making rude signs at the man as he screeched away. Putting the brake on the cart, she jumped down and tried to soothe Parly, who was wide-eyed and frightened, jumping, sweating and foaming.

Arthur jumped down from the cart, too, to inspect the damage. "The wheel's cracked," he said reluctantly in the ensuing silence. "I don't think it will hold up." As he crouched to look at it, there came the sound of more approaching engines. Rufus barked and jumped out of the cart.

"Oh no," breathed Maria. "Not more."

"Motorbikes, by the sound of it," said Arthur, grabbing Rufus' collar and he was right. There were five of them, like giant bees zooming along towards them. The noise reminded Maria of the planes and she scanned the empty sky fearfully. Maybe this will be it, she thought, holding Parly close and closing her eyes. Now the motorbikes were wild animals, gaining on them and they were the prey.

She gritted her teeth and waited for the pain of the first bite as the posse of black noise and energy flashed deafeningly by, centimetres away – one, two, three, four, five. Parly gave a terrified neigh and tried to bolt. It was all Maria could do to stay on her feet and hold on to the reins. Then, as quickly as the band of faceless riders had come, they had gone.

"The cart!" yelled Arthur suddenly as the last vestige of screaming metal receded in the distance. "The wheel's cracking! It's going over!" Arthur put his back to the cart to hold it up. For a second, Maria was frozen to the spot. "Get Parly free, I won't be able to hold it for long!" Arthur yelled.

The urgency in his voice made Maria move. She ran to free Parly from the harness, but the faster she tried to work, the slower her fingers seemed to move. She wanted to stamp and yell, but knew she needed to calm her terrified horse. Outwardly she spoke reassuringly to Parly; inwardly she screamed obscenities.

"Hurry up!" called Arthur desperately, straining with his back to the cart. "We've got to get Emily out, too!" But just as Maria finally walked a jumpy, frightened Parly free of the cart, the damaged wheel gave way with a loud crack. Arthur leaped out of the way as the cart tipped over towards him. Everything slid out, including Emily, who didn't so much as whimper; she just rolled out on to the road like a piece of luggage.

"Emily!" screamed Maria. She tied Parly to the five-bar gate at the entrance to the field, then rushed to her sister, who was lying in the middle of the road, surrounded by bags, rugs, carrots and apples. Arthur was already there. Together, he and Maria carried her to the grassy verge behind the cart. Her eyes didn't open. She was breathing heavily and noisily, but they couldn't wake her up. She was unconscious. Maria wailed a long, desperate, "No!" Rufus whined and tried to lick away the tears, but she just let them keep falling as she knelt beside her sister on the muddy grass. Emily was dying. Now what were they going to do? How were they going to get her to Dad now? Maybe Dad wasn't even alive himself . . . Maria howled in agony. She felt more lost and alone than she knew it was possible to be.

"We need a miracle," admitted Arthur softly, running his fingers anxiously through his short, black hair. Maria didn't answer. There was no answer. She tucked herself into a ball and rocked and cried until there were no tears left and all that remained in the pit of her soul was a dull emptiness.

At last Maria sat up. Emily was still breathing; Rufus was sitting with her, whining and nudging her from time to time with his wet nose, but still she didn't move. The wind was ruffling her dull, lifeless hair and her new jacket was pattered with streaks of mud, but at least she was still alive. Maria wiped away the remaining dampness from her tear-streaked face, stood up and looked disinterestedly around. She felt as though her life had been drained away and all that was left was the shell. The cart lay half in the road, half on the narrow verge, broken and useless, but somehow it didn't matter. Nothing mattered any more. It was as if she was watching some weird, Italian film, the sort that had no real ending. Arthur was collecting up the last of the apples from the road into a sack.

"Better go," he suggested quietly, turning and seeing her watching him. Maria looked at him with big, empty, solemn eyes, but didn't answer. An empty coke can broke the silence, rattling along the old, grey tarmac in the breeze.

"We'll find some people. Any people," Arthur said at last, "except van drivers. Get some help." A tatty magazine flapped around the broken cartwheel. Maria nodded and raised her stiff, aching body from the verge. She tried to muster some enthusiasm and make her brain work. Yes, they needed help. They couldn't manage on their own any longer. They didn't know where they were going, or if it was even worth it. She leaned over the gate to the field, half-expecting to see someone walking towards her, but there was no sign of life – only a field of grass, then trees, then more fields; they could have been just about anywhere in Kent, or even on an uninhabited planet somewhere, made to look like Kent.

Maria turned round. "I suppose we'll have to carry Emily between us, somehow," she sighed. "Leave Parly here."

"Couldn't Emily ride her?"

"Don't be an idiot, Arthur, she can't hold on!" snapped Maria. Trust Arthur to suggest something stupid.

"You could ride with her," persisted Arthur. "It's got to be possible! There must be a way . . ." his voice trailed away. Maria slowly, tiredly, considered his suggestion, but almost immediately dismissed it. Parly was big enough and strong enough to carry the two of them, but they had no saddle nor stirrups.

"How can I hold on to Emily and the reins at the same time?" she sighed. She shuddered involuntarily. "We'd slide off – smash every bone in our bodies!"

"Sure," nodded Arthur soothingly. "You're right. Never mind, we won't leave the poor horse for long – we'll come back for her, as soon as possible, won't we?" Maria grimaced and turned away, feeling new tears rising unbidden to her eyes again. "You're going to France, remember?"

Dumping the apples, Arthur walked over to her and put a gentle hand on her shoulder. "Maria, we'll make it yet," he whispered. His hand felt strong, yet warm and soothing. Maria felt his quiet strength and the warmth of his companionship. Angels, she thought suddenly. They still had granny's angels. She allowed a tiny new ray of hope to creep into her heart.

"I've got it!" yelled Arthur suddenly, gripping her shoulder. "We'll make a stretcher for Emily out of one of the sacks! He tipped out the apples and carrots he had just collected, but his enthusiasm quickly flickered and died. "It's not big enough," he admitted reluctantly, staring at the sack. "Or strong enough." He fiddled with the length of rope, seeking inspiration, but it was useless. Maria half-watched, knowing that it wouldn't work.

"Do you want me to go and look for help?" asked Arthur suddenly, sounding like he had been thinking of it, but had put off asking. Maria didn't answer. She had been thinking the same thing, but she didn't want him to go either. Tears welled up in her eyes. Without replying, she walked back over to the fence and slouched over the gate. It wasn't fair. Then, suddenly, she stared at the view in a new way. Her heart began to beat faster. Surely that big old oak tree in the field beyond was the one that she and Emily used to climb when they were little? And that spire, just poking out above the trees at the far edge of the field was a familiar spire, surely? With a sudden surge of energy, Maria scrambled up on to the wreck of the cart to get a better view. As far as she could remember she had never been down this lane, just seen it from the branches of the old tree. But it was that tree. And it was the spire of the church where she had been christened.

"Our cottage is over there!" she screamed, wildly indicating the direction. "Just over there, through the trees!"

twenty-nine

Grandpa and Mum had been out searching for the girls when Maria banged on the cottage door, but Granny had come running. Maria had nearly broken the door down; Granny hadn't known whether to laugh or cry when she opened it and saw her granddaughters there, dirty and dishevelled, one of whom was out cold and being carried by an unknown young man with a dog. But Dad, who had been digging in the back garden, had known exactly what to do. While Granny got down on her knees and prayed, joined, to her surprise and joy by Arthur, Dad had given Emily two injections and set up an intravenous drip, which he hung from a coat and hat stand by her bed. "I knew these would come in useful," he murmured to himself, as he worked. It was difficult for Maria to leave Emily, even with Dad and Granny, but they couldn't leave Parly where she was in the road, so she and Arthur ran back for her. By the time the horse was safe in the paddock, Emily had come round enough to recognise Dad and take a few sips of water. They had all cried, even Dad.

Then, before Maria had had time to introduce Arthur, Rufus and Parly properly, Mum and Grandpa had returned. Maria stared at her mother as she came through the door; she had changed so much. She was thinner, her face was pale, her lips drawn and her arm was in a sling. "Maria," whispered her mum, rooted to the spot. "Is that you?" Maria couldn't remember the last time she had hugged her mum; it seemed both odd and perfectly normal at the same time, which was weird.

"Mind your mother's arm," warned Dad. "I'm afraid she's had an accident." Maria grimaced, remembering the surgery. But at least she was alive.

Then there was a flurry of activity and more tears as Grandpa and Mum heard about Emily and went up to her bedside, where Granny was keeping vigil.

After that, a calm descended on the cottage and the cheerfulness that comes with relief. Mum sat with Emily while Granny made a cup of tea, Arthur shook hands with everyone and charmed them with his dazzling smile and Rufus made them all laugh by offering his paw for everyone to shake, too.

Mum had her tea with Emily upstairs; everyone else sat in the lounge. Peace, at last, began to replace the tension and fear that had dogged Maria for so long. The nightmare of the last few days, culminating with carrying Emily to the cottage across the field and paddock, was beginning to recede, as dreams do when morning comes. Everyone was alive! Parly was safe in the paddock, Rufus was sitting on her feet and the hot tea, though made with powdered milk, was the best she had ever tasted. She closed her eyes, took a deep breath and let it out in a slow sigh, sinking further down into the upholstery of the plush settee. What a luxury after the hard seat of that bumpy cart!

"I'm very proud of you, Maria, my dear," declared Granny, placing a tray of cookies and fruit cake on a little table. "You've done marvellously, coming all this way on your own and looking after Emily. And we're very grateful to you, Arthur, too," she added, her eyes twinkling in his direction.

"You prayed for angels to look after us," said Maria unexpectedly. "I think they did." Arthur grinned broadly at her and Granny and Grandpa both nodded.

"Well now!" said Grandpa. "Did you see them?"

Maria looked at him in surprise, then saw the twinkle in his eye. She grinned and was just about to retort, "No, of course not," when she remembered Rufus and Arthur. "Maybe . . ." she replied instead.

"Well, God always answers our prayers," interjected Granny. "Not always in the way we expect him to, I'll admit, but we can always trust him, because he knows best."

"Very true," nodded Grandpa. "Take, for example, that horse and cart. That was very kind of the owner to lend them to you, with Emily unwell." Maria and Arthur exchanged an uneasy glance.

"When do you have to take them back?" added Dad.

Maria narrowed her eyes at her father. "We're never taking them back! They come from Parlingworth House; it used to be a National Heritage place. We stayed there last night. But it's been taken over by an evil man now."

"An evil man?" asked Dad immediately, sitting up.

"What's this about an evil man?"

"Oh dear," murmured Granny.

Maria concentrated on swirling the tea in her cup. She didn't want to talk about it. Not yet. She didn't even want to think about it.

Granny seemed to understand. "Tell us about it when you're ready," she suggested kindly.

"No exaggerating, mind!" added Grandpa, with the usual twinkle in his eye. She would hardly need to exaggerate. Leave things out, more like. But her dad obviously had some more questions. Oh no, thought Maria grimly, seeing the look in his eyes that annoyed her, before he even opened his mouth.

"What I don't understand is why you didn't leave us a note to say you'd left," he said, in the irritatingly superior tone that Maria hated. "I don't know where you've been hiding but we've just about scoured the whole of Kent looking for you! If you had only told us . . ."

Maria glared fiercely back. "We did leave a note," she interrupted hotly. "But we didn't come straight to the cottage, we went to look for you at Granny and Grandpa's."

"Don't give me that nonsense! We would have seen you!"

"Well you didn't!" Maria replied fiercely. "Ask Mrs Fitchett, we saw her! And what *I* don't understand is why *you* didn't come home when you said you would!" Only the sound of the old clock ticking on the mantelpiece and a saucepan lid rattling in the kitchen could be heard in the following, uneasy silence.

Granny and Grandpa looked at each other. Dad cleared his throat. "Why didn't you just get out? You must have listened to the radio! You knew that our area was being evacuated?"

Maria stared at him. "I didn't listen to the radio. I didn't know," she admitted.

Dad took a deep breath and stared at his slice of fruitcake. "No, no, of course you didn't. And of course, I forget, there were the burglars too . . ."

"We didn't see them," admitted Maria. "They came after we left."

"Well that's one good thing," sighed Dad. The antagonism was fading now; he just sounded tired. "I'm sorry, Maria, I shouldn't blame you. I'm sorry we took so long, yes, yes, of course it must have been very frightening for you, waiting for us. We did think of you. I'm afraid we got delayed at the surgery." He hesitated a little and sighed. "You may as well know the truth. You needn't tell your sister, but a mob of rough youths wanted drugs from the surgery. They stole my keys, along with some other things and locked your mother and me in the seminar room. To put it mildly, there was a fight. I'm afraid they ransacked the place. And they shot your mother – in the arm. Driving down here was very difficult," he added with a sigh. "She's going to be all right," he added quickly, in the silence that followed this announcement.

"We saw the surgery," Maria managed to say airily, swallowing hard at the thought of her mother's arm. "When we went to look for you. We saw Mum's handbag all covered in blood." Granny covered her mouth with her hand and Grandpa shook his head gravely.

"Oh dear, did you?" answered Dad, wincing. "I'm sorry about that, terribly sorry. That must have been an awful shock. Anyway, to cut a long story short, a passer-by let us out next morning." Maria nodded. It didn't seem shocking, now, in an odd sort of way. It just seemed like another lifetime away, almost a dream.

"And about our note," said Maria loftily, "the reason you didn't see it was because the burglars chucked it on the floor with the stuff from the bureau – I found it there when we got back. We got yours, though, Granny, thank you," she added pointedly, smiling at her Granny. "You didn't see us," she added to her father, "but we saw you when we got back home – you were disappearing off down the road." She paused for effect. "We shouted, but you didn't stop."

Granny breathed in sharply, Dad stared and Grandpa exclaimed, "Well I never!"

Maria looked at the floor and tried to sound a bit pathetic. She might as well make the most of the moment. "Was it you who took all the food, Dad?" she asked. She could sense Arthur grinning, but managed not to look at him. He had got to know her well in the last few days.

Her dad sounded really upset this time. "Why yes, we did."

Granny took another sharp breath. "I can hardly believe it!" she exclaimed. "Fancy coming back to find we'd gone and left you nothing to eat! You poor dears! So what have you been living on?"

Maria used a little silence to what she hoped would be

her benefit, deciding not to mention that everything they had eaten they had stolen. "Well, it hasn't been easy," she sighed, "but as you see, we're still here. I think I probably have lost a bit of weight." She tried to pinch around her waist, thinking quickly, not daring to look at Arthur. Now would be a good time to bring up the subject of Rufus. "I can keep my dog, can't I?" she asked beseechingly. She lowered her voice and shuddered as if remembering something awful. "Once when a drunk jumped out on Emily, Rufus saved her." Dad stared at her as if his eyes would pop out of his head and Grandpa and Granny gave exclamations of horror.

Maria waited anxiously for the answer to her request, not daring to speak. Rufus was still sitting on her feet, his dear head resting against her knee, enjoying all the attention. She scratched his head and he looked up at her lovingly. Maria leaned down to give him a hug, smelly though he was and he licked her face. Surely that must make the cutest picture, she thought, surely that would melt even her dad's heart?

"Well . . ." said Dad at last.

"A guard dog would be jolly useful," nodded Grandpa. Maria held her breath.

"Well, all right, Maria," agreed Dad, "but you'll have to give him a bath and he's not to go upstairs, or on the furniture. We'll see if he's micro-chipped as and when. And I can see there's going to be a lot of explaining to do, on both sides, in the next few days." Maria looked up. She had played that one nicely, but still, she hadn't expected it to be that easy. She grinned at her father and he smiled back. "You've earned your dog, love," he added gently. Maria's eyes swam. Her father had smiled at her and called her "love"!

"Such a lovely dog, too," agreed Granny. "And I'm so sorry we took all the food from the house. I still can't believe we left you with nothing!"

"Well," sighed Maria dramatically, making the most of her celebrity status, "we did find a couple of bagels." At last she caught Arthur's eye. He stifled a cough. But Maria knew she was on to a winning streak and had to make the most of the moment. "And Parly?" she wheedled, dabbing her eyes, trying to ignore Arthur.

Dad pursed his lips as if trying to think of a way to get out of that one and Maria waited with baited breath. "I've got an idea there," said Grandpa. "How about we consider them to be on loan, then when the National Heritage sets up again we can take them back, well-looked after. I'll have a go at fixing that broken wheel. Does that sound fair? To be honest, they could come in useful if petrol runs out." Everybody nodded, even Dad. And, thought Maria delightedly to herself, there would be plenty of time later to argue about keeping Parly permanently and Rufus, never mind the micro-chip.

Arthur couldn't help himself any longer and laughed out loud, then obviously feeling that some explanation for the laughter was required, changed the subject quickly. "You should have seen Maria fixing Parly to the cart with all the reins and straps and collar," he said. "She was fantastic!"

"Well, it's no more than I would have expected of our

Maria, my dear," agreed Granny, nodding, handing round the plate of cake again. "There's no doubt about it; you were all just marvellous and very brave. And thank God, with your dad here to look after her, I'm sure Emily will be better soon too."

Maria plumped up her cushion and looked round at her father and grandparents. Granny and Grandpa's smiles still shone out from their friendly, wrinkled faces, but in a strange way, her dad somehow looked older than them. More careworn. Maria felt that she had grown up a lot over the last few days, too. It was something inside, something she couldn't explain.

"Well, I'm sorry things didn't turn out the way we hoped," sighed Dad. "I'm sorry you had to come all this way alone. But now we'll stay here for a while. It may be that things will settle down quickly and we'll all get back to normal, but we have to be prepared for the worst. According to the radio, the threat of war isn't over yet. Grandpa and I have been cleaning out the old well. It's a bit of a messy job," he added ruefully, staring at his soiled plaster cast. "But at least then we'll have fresh water. And in the paddock – well, we were going to start growing vegetables, but now you've brought a horse . . ."

"We can eat that instead!" twinkled Grandpa.

"Grandpa!" laughed Maria as she shot a cushion in his direction. "Nobody's ever going to eat Parly!" Rufus started barking and grabbed the cushion.

"Mind your tea!" barked Dad.

* * *

Maria lay awake for a long time that night, unable to sleep. Rufus was taking up a lot of room on her bed and Arthur was leaving in the morning; she knew that she would miss him badly. But something else was bothering her, now that she had time to think. Everything had seemed so safe here when she had first arrived, but was it just an illusion? How long could the cottage shield them from the world outside? Maria thought of the lack of signposts, of Mr Oliver "taking over this part of the country" and her father's warning that the threat of war was not yet over. Then there was the unthinkable problem of running out of food and water. Plus, her mother didn't look so good and Emily was far from well yet.

Just after two in the morning, Maria gave up the fight to sleep and padded over to her little bedroom window in the eaves. Pushing open the old, black, metal frame, she curled up on the window seat, wrapping her soft dressing gown around her feet for warmth. Rufus came and sat with her, resting his head on her knee and looking up with his melting, brown eyes. The cool, green, mingling scents of the garden and the countryside beyond wafted in. Stars studded the dark sky and the moon shone round and bright, bathing everything in gentle shadows, as it had last night at Parlingworth House. Maria breathed in the still night air. It was quiet outside, almost too quiet, as if the world was poised, holding its breath, waiting for something to happen.

Then Maria suddenly realised that her journey to the cottage was not an end, it was a beginning. This was what she had waited to understand, what she needed to know.

Now that she knew, she felt less afraid. For as Maria allowed the soft air from the open window to touch her bare face and hands, it felt like a gentle caress from an unseen world, like angels' wings. Maybe, reflected Maria, there was someone out there who would take care of her, whatever happened.

She went back to bed. Tomorrow was another day. London was gone, but there were other things that still remained. Angels, it seemed, were one of them.